TERTULLIAN OF AFRICA

THE RHETORIC OF A NEW AGE

QUINCY HOWE, PHD

iUniverse, Inc.
Bloomington

Tertullian of Africa
The Rhetoric of a New Age

iUniverse books may be ordered through booksellers or by contacting:

iUniverse
1663 Liberty Drive
Bloomington, IN 47403
www.iuniverse.com
1-800-Authors (1-800-288-4677)

ISBN: 978-1-4620-6452-6 (sc)
ISBN: 978-1-4620-6453-3 (ebk)

Printed in the United States of America

iUniverse rev. date: 01/06/2012

INTRODUCTION

THE LIFE OF TERTULLIAN

Tertullian's life is not a dramatic story consisting of major assignments, positions, and accomplishments. His personal narrative can be reduced to a single sentence: He was an exceptional writer of great prolixity and originality. The available facts are few in number and often subject to debate.

He was born in the city of Carthage around 160 AD. The Carthaginians fought three major wars with the Romans and their city was destroyed by Scipio Africanus in 146 BC. This is important information because it places Carthage at a unique position in Roman history. In the pre-Christian era Carthage had been Rome's most menacing enemy. In the Christian era it was the country of origin for Tertullian, St. Cyprian, and St. Augustine, all three of them major forces in the emergence of the Catholic faith. The classical tradition, launched by writers such as Virgil, Cicero, Quintillian, and Seneca did not feed into the formation of Christian thought. As the classical tradition was fading, these African successors from Rome's ancient enemy launched the wording and perception of reality that became western Christianity.

I can provide no more than a couple of facts about Tertullian and the works I am translating. They are *Ad Nationes I, To the Nations Book I* composed in 197 AD and *De Testimonio Animae, On the Testimony of the Soul.,* composed in 197-98 AD.

There is no evidence that he was raised as a Christian, which leads to the surmise that he was a convert. He was married and it is evident from his writings that his wife was also Christian. There is some debate about his training. He clearly had ample rhetorical training. He was also very familiar with judicial procedure; however, this was true of rhetoricians in general. There are intimations that he may have been a priest, but no more than intimations.

Later in life he drifted away from mainstream Christianity and became a Montanist, a Christian sect that attached extreme significance to the power of the Holy Spirit. The general consensus is that Tertullian did not actually abandon Christianity. These are the salient known facts about the life of Tertullian.

TERTULLIAN AS A WRITER

Tertullian is an extraordinary presence both in the history of Christian thought and in the development of Latin prose. He wrote about Christianity and its pagan critics with an immediacy that was evident from his earliest works. Tertullian is rumored to have advanced to considerable old age. There are those who like to surmise that he lived as late as 249 AD. On the other hand, to judge by his writings, which end in 222 AD, he would have lived at least to the age of sixty-two. There are thirty-one extant works attributed to Tertullian. These are polemics, eulogies, and a broad range of cultural essays. As I hope to make evident from the two works I am offering in translation, he writes with fervor and ease. These two pieces were written largely for pagan instruction. The pagans were persecuting the Christians both for their reported vices and their unwillingness to accord to the Emperor the vow of unswerving loyalty.

As for the reported vices of the Christians, Tertullian takes deep pleasure in exercising his vexation and incredulity of the vices that had become associated with the Christian name. There were rumors of incest, infanticide, and dining on pieces of bread dripping with human blood. And Tertullian presents them with vividness and a sense of dismissive mockery. The reader is drawn into the position to reflect on how the devout new Christian, willing to die for his faith, could possibly engage in these vices associated with the Christian faith while rejoicing in the promise of Resurrection and God's unfailing forgiveness.

A major driving forces behind Tertullian's style is the rhetorical movement known as the Second Sophistic, which was flourishing toward the end of the second century AD. The devices at his disposal are irony, paradox, and sarcasm. In his essay *On the Testimony of the Soul,* Tertullian finds himself in touch with a resource, namely his soul, which operates through direct disclosure rather than through the labored convolutions of the mind.

One of Tertullian's cherished assumptions is that the pagans, despite their persecution of the Christians and their relentless disapproval of Christian vices, have a profound affinity with the Christians. If they could just set aside their harangues against the reported vices, they might recognize that the pagans and the Christians occupy a common ground. Despite the persecutions and the judicial accusations of flagrant Christian malfeasance, the pagans need to view the Christian position with some of the irony and paradox that permeate the Second Sophistic.

In the pages that follow I am presenting translations supported by commentary that should draw attention to the common ground available to all in second century Carthage.

In the midst of these tumultuous and menacing realities, Tertullian produced a body of work that is unique in its presentation of Christian belief. What I would like to attempt in this study is to single out those features of the Christian experience that most immediately and persuasively moved Tertullian. I am including only two works: *On the Testimony of the Soul* and *Ad Nationes.Book I.* The first of these is characterized by an attitude of worshipful reverence—not a recurrent posture in Tertullian. *Ad Nationes* is a diminutive specimen of Tertullian's most forceful work, *The Apology*. In both the *Apology* and the *ad Nationes* Tertullian belabors the myriad paradoxes and contradictions that arise from the pagan assault on Christianity. Tertullian is aware of the many ways in which the pagans are appropriate candidates for Christian conversion.

I will start with *On the Testimony of the Soul* where Tertullian tries to explain what has provided both the evidence and the assurances that sustain his Christian belief. As he quotes what he takes to be the spontaneous self-disclosures of his soul, we must remain mindful of the fact that Tertullian is writing at a time when the soul did not have self-evident access to inspired and revealed truth. He is constrained by the intimations, perceptions, and reflections that come to him as the spontaneous expressions of his soul.

Another source of inspiration for Tertullian was the realization that the Christians had been summoned to embrace a truth that demanded the ultimate sacrifice and delivered ultimate benediction. There is a very considerable body of writing among the early Church fathers about the sacrifice and sanctity of the martyrs. For the Christian who may be experiencing a moment of dejection and apprehension, there is in Tertullian's famous line, "*Cristianus ad leonem*" (Christian to the lion) a shudder of reassuring defiance.

A further aspect of Tertullian that needs to be addressed in any attempt to create a literary study is his labored legacy as a man of letters. In the judgment of Eduard Norden, the most authoritative critic of Latin prose, Tertullian is the most difficult Latin writer. This assessment is in fact a fair estimate and has had a great impact on Tertullian scholarship. His translators take extreme pains to show that they understand his meaning. As a consequence these translations are often done at the expense of fluent and graceful expression. A further consequence of Tertullian's flamboyant and elaborately crafted prose style is that the scholars and critics who have chosen him as their subject have assumed a rigid posture of scrupulous exactitude. As with the translators, this scrupulosity is done as a precautionary measure against being misled by Tertullian's vigorous frivolity, but this too exacts a price in terms of grace and fluency.

I am hoping to find myself caught up in a style of thought and expression that does justice to the excitement, vigor, and spiritual urgency that pervade Tertullian's writing.

I wish to thank Dr. R. Kevin Johnson and Dr. Richard K. Fadem for their editorial acuity in assisting with the preparation of this book.

CONTENTS

CHAPTER 1

THE AUTHORITY OF THE SOUL

There are moments in history when the self-understanding of a civilization is subject to major change. These moments will occur in response to new circumstances whose scope and novelty lie beyond the immediate vocabulary to account for what is taking place. The rise of Christianity in North Africa was such an occurrence and Tertullian was one of the leading figures in this pivotal transformation.

He was an enormously prolific and accomplished writer whose legacy is a controversial body of work that has attracted admiration and exasperation. He wrote apology, polemic, theology, defamation of the pagans, and defamation of the heretics. Of immediate interest is *On the Testimony of the Soul*, where he endeavored to launch a convincing personal vehicle to convey his perception of Christian truth. There are many ways to approach the writings of Tertullian and there are occasions when he is laboring in a strictly confessional mode. *On the Testimony of the Soul* is one such occasion. He is greatly at ease with sarcasm, irony, paradox, and contradiction—all of which draw the reader away from the worshipful and reverent conviction that can be found in his confessional writing. The problem facing any North African convert to Christianity from the patristic period—whether it is Tertullian or St. Augustine—is the availability of a convincing and recognized style with which to express one's personal Christian belief. In this essay Tertullian creates for himself an immediate ally whom he invokes as "the testimony of the soul."

In Tertullian's hands, the Testimony of the Soul turns out to be those exclamations that people—all people—use to acknowledge God. This essay seeks to isolate and identify Tertullian's linguistic usage when he is trying to express something for which there is as yet no established method of exposition. One of the extraordinary realities that presents itself to the reader of Tertullian is how well he is able to convey his fervor, his conviction, and his enthusiasm for a cause that is at the very inception of making its presence known.

Great curiosity, and an even greater gift of memory, will be required of anyone who seeks to draw evidence of Christian truth from the most popular works of the philosophers, the poets, or the masters of worldly learning and wisdom—particularly if this is being undertaken to convict our rivals and enemies of error on their own behalf and injustice toward us Christians. There are, in fact, those in whom an intensity of curiosity and persistence of memory have prevailed. They have placed at our disposal works in this vein where they recall and present in detail the reasoning, sources, traditions, and arguments through which it becomes clear that we have launched nothing novel nor ominous. In this respect, we Christians require no support from popular and public letters to ensure that we reject error and embrace justice. The natural stubbornness of humankind has subverted faith even in your most esteemed and outstanding teachers whenever they have advanced plausible arguments in behalf of Christianity. Your poets are misinformed when they endow the gods with human passions and portray them in fanciful stories. The philosophers are obtuse when they knock at the doors of truth. One is considered wise and sensible only as long as his declarations are merely approximately Christian. But if he has set his heart upon wisdom and enlightenment while rejecting this pagan world, he is branded as a Christian. We want nothing to do with a literature and body of instruction that espouses false happiness by advocating what is false rather than what is true.

The above paragraph launches Tertullian's treatise and provides a vivid and telling picture of where the author finds himself in the year 198 AD. He is a recent convert to Christianity and he is writing at a time when declaring a belief in Christianity was to risk execution. The Christians were unwilling to acknowledge the divinity of the Emperor, which was to declare oneself the enemy of the world order inhabited by your fellow citizens. Among Tertullian's concerns on behalf of Christian believers was to make it clear there was nothing novel nor ominous in their beliefs. As a consequence, Christians need to be alert to avoid any menacing or apocalyptic view of pagan reality. A further problem facing the Christians is the inherent distance between their theistic and worshipful view of Christian reality as compared with the mythic and fanciful vision of reality that envelops the pagan gods.

Let us acknowledge that there are those pagans who have declared in favor of the one true God. Better that nothing were declared that a Christian might accept, lest he turn it as a reproach against the pagans. Not everyone knows what the pagans have declared nor do those who do know have full faith in what they know. It is even more improbable that readers are assenting to works of ours to which no one has access unless he is already a Christian.

In some respects Carthage of the second century was similar to our present world. The spiritual and intellectual landscape was changing with great rapidity and the distribution of power was in flux. Any endeavor at such a time to provide an objective account of what is actually taking place is fraught with difficulty and ambiguity. By Tertullian's account, the pagan poets and philosophers are misinformed about the nature of spiritual reality. They attribute to the pagan gods the same passions, excesses, and misguided suppositions that afflicted the entire pagan world.

As the authoritative measure of reality Tertullian settled on the human soul. In his analysis of the soul he expresses himself with no assurance provided by any traditional body of learning. Any attempt to pin down the exact nature of the soul consists of little more than a casual nod toward Plato, Epicurus, or the Stoics. After evading any specific indication as to the origin or intrinsic nature of the soul, he closes the section with one of his most famous lines. "As far as I know, you (sc. the soul) are not inherently Christian. The soul can become Christian but it is not born Christian."

Tertullian is often apprehensive of offending the pagans by making presumptuous claims on behalf of Christian primacy. To assert that the soul is born Christian could offend a pagan believer in Plato, Epicurus or the Stoics. Pagan philosophy leaves ample space for the soul; but for Tertullian to assert that the soul is born Christian is to enter a space that has already been spoken for by pagan philosophy. To allow for the possibility of the soul becoming Christian invites the possibility that the soul, which is the defining essence of mankind, can make the passage into Christian belief.

Now I invoke a new witness better known than any literature—more compelling than any theory, more widely circulated than any publication, greater than the fullness of man—the very sum of man. O soul, step forth into our midst, whether you are divine and eternal as many philosophers attest. All the more would you (the soul) not lie! Or whether you are not divine, since you are material as only Epicurus suggests. Then all the more you ought not to lie. Whether you are received from heaven or conceived from the earth; whether you are assembled from numbers or atoms; whether you originate with the body; whether you are introduced into the body after birth. However you originate, you make of mankind a rational animal, supremely receptive to awareness and knowledge.

I do not summon you as one formed by schooling, instructed by libraries, nurtured by Platonic and Stoic academies that you may trumpet your wisdom. I invoked you in your simple, unfinished, untutored, unformed nature—such as you are for those who have only you alone. Such as you are at the crossroads, on the street, in the workshop. I need you in your innocence since no one trusts even the smallest measure of your experience. I demand of you those primal sparks you confer on man, those insights that you have learned from your own depths or from your creator, whoever he may be. As far as I know, you are not inherently Christian. The soul can become Christian; but it is not born Christian. Christians are now demanding evidence from you to be presented to your adversaries from without so that those may blush before you who have hated and mocked us for the very beliefs that they now discover you have always known.

A recurrent theme in Tertullian's thought is the provocative notion that when the pagans harangue against Christianity, they are, in fact, expressing misconceptions the falsity of which would be apparent to them if they could just subject themselves to greater rigor and closer scrutiny of their own thoughts.

CHAPTER II

THE SOUL INVOKES CHRISTIAN TRUTH

The opening sentence of this section addresses the pagan objections to the Christian monotheistic vision of an all-powerful God. The pagans generally maintained a rather defensive passion on behalf of their polytheism. The monotheistic notion does not leave permissive space for the possibility of the numerous pagan gods who may suddenly feel diminished or threatened by a single, all-powerful Christian God.

We are deemed offensive when we preach the one God under one name from whom and under whom everything exists. Give witness, O my soul, if such is your conviction. For we hear you pagans proclaiming openly and with full freedom—such as is never granted to us at home and abroad—"May God grant it," or "If God wills it." With these words you indicate that God exists and you concede all power to him. You are subject to his will and yet at the same time you deny that the others are gods since you address them by their traditional names such as Saturn, Jove, Mars, Minerva.

> This chapter enters a new arena in the progress of thought. The tone is now distinctly theistic in the sense that the word **Deus** (God) is used to indicate the supreme godhead, as in Christian scripture. Thus, when the soul invokes the name of God in this section it does so with characteristically Christian reverence. When the soul proclaims "May God grant it," or "if God wills it," it is set free from the primitive and mythic mentality of the pagans who address God by such fanciful names such as Jove, Mars, Minerva.

You pagans confirm that he alone is God whom you address as God. When you occasionally refer to the others as "God," you appear to be using the term in a displaced and borrowed sense. The nature of the God whom we preach does not escape you. You claim, "God is good," or "God is bountiful." Clearly you are implying "But man is evil." With this reversal of meaning you are suggesting indirectly and figuratively that man has departed from the good God.

Since every blessing from the God of goodness and kindness is for us the consummate sacrament of doctrine and discourse, you exclaim, "May God bless you" as readily befits a Christian. But when you convert your blessing into a curse, you are admitting according to us that God holds all power over us.

There are those who, even though they do not deny God, do not think of him as the final witness, arbiter, and judge. In this respect they are profoundly at odds with us who take refuge in this belief in fear of the threat of condemnation. They thus honor God by releasing him from the toil of keeping watch and unloading the burden of punishment. They do not even attribute anger to him for they say that, if God is capable of anger, he is then subject to corruption and passion. What is corruptible and passionate is therefore subject to annihilation, which cannot touch God.

But elsewhere, confessing that the soul is divine or bestowed by God, you stumble against the testimony of the soul itself thus refuting the prior notion. If the soul is divine or bestowed by God, then without doubt, it knows its own creator and, knowing this, fears him as its ultimate resource. And does it not then fear the one whose good will is preferable to his wrath? How can there be a natural fear of the soul toward God if God does not know rage? How can one be feared, if he cannot take offense? What is to be feared if not wrath itself? What gives rise to wrath if not outrage? What provokes outrage if not judgment? What enables judgment if not power? And in whom is all power vested if not in God alone?

Hence, O soul, it is accorded to you to proclaim from your own awareness, at home and abroad, no one mocking, no one objecting, "God sees all." "I trust in God." "God will make it good." "God will judge between us." How does this come to you, O soul, if you are not Christian?

When your gods are bound in the ribbon of Ceres, when clad in the scarlet pallium of Saturn, when robed in the linen gown of Isis, when in the very temples of the gods, O soul, you often call upon God as your judge. You stand at the feet of Asclepius, you adorn the brazen image of Juno, and you decorate the helmet of Minerva with dark omens. And yet while doing this, you do not invoke the god you are addressing. In your own forum you summon a judge from beyond. In your temples you experience an alien divinity. O testimony of truth which conjures up a Christian witness in the midst of these pagan demons!

Tertullian begins to move toward a realization that the willingness to assent to Christian belief is not something that comes as the revelation of a superior reality. Rather it is something that emerges naturally from the soul's cumulative grasp of Christianity. When the pagans find themselves in a worshipful stance before their own divinities, they are using the name of the Lord in what Tertullian refers to in this chapter as "a displaced and borrowed sense." The last line of the above section is in profound alignment with Tertullian's thinking. When the pagans engage in worship of their gods—Ceres,

Saturn, Isis—they are in direct proximity to Christian practice. The soul will proclaim, "God sees all. God makes it good." The challenge that Tertullian is laying before the pagans at this point is to recognize that they do not recognize the god they are addressing. They are also being urged to recognize that when they are engaged in their worship, the soul is offering a testimony of truth that conjures up a Christian witness, namely God.

CHAPTER III

THE SOUL IS CAPABLE OF

CHOOSING DAMNATION

This chapter is essentially an appendage to chapter two, affirming that knowledge of God naturally implies knowledge of Satan. Since we spontaneously refer to people as demons when they indulge in hateful behavior, it must follow that the soul is also acquainted with the "Angel of evil." Placing Satan in the soul's store of instinctive knowledge, Tertullian makes brief but explicit reference to damnation and estrangement from God. It is conceivable at this point that the thoughtful but resistant pagan might stop to ponder whether the recognition of "demonic" flaws in our fellow humans leads inevitably to the reality of Satan and the ensuing fall of man from God's favor. In the resourceful hands of Tertullian this generic and spontaneous soul is now making rapid progress toward becoming a comprehensive messenger of Christian doctrine.

When we assert that demons exist, some follower of Chrysippus[1] will sneer at us—as if we did not in fact prove they exist since we alone can cast them out.[2] Your curses confirm that they exist and that they are the object of loathing. You will call a person a demon who is flawed by indecency or malice or arrogance or whatever odious defect we attribute to demons. Satan, whom we call the angel of evil, you pagans invoke to express shock, contempt, or loathing. He is the architect of all error, the corrupter of the entire world by whom man was defrauded from the beginning that he might transgress the command of the Lord. As a result man is now given over to death and has made his entire progeny the vehicle of damnation now infected by his own seed. Therefore you know your downfall and only those know him who are Christians or have abided by the word of the Lord. Nevertheless, you know him, for you have hated him.

---

[1]   Chrysippus (280-207 BC) was a Stoic philosopher who in fact asserted that there were both good and evil demons.

[2]   At the time of Tertullian one of the pagan suppositions about Christians was that they were uniquely endowed with the gift of being able to cast out demons. It is evident in this passage that by Tertullian's account, the reality of damnation and estrangement are primal elements of the Christian experience.

CHAPTER IV

THE POST-MORTEM EXISTENCE OF THE

SOUL

Continuing to draw on the testimony of the soul, Tertullian proceeds to develop a theory of the afterlife with rewards or punishments accorded to the merits of life in this world. By Tertullian's account, the soul cannot experience the afterlife unless it is reunited with the specific body through which the life experiences took place. Implicit in this vision of an afterlife is the resurrection of the body. Unlike the Ātman of Vedanta or the psyche of Platonism, the soul as conceived by Tertullian is not capable of a disincarnate existence. The soul retains a significant imprint from its corporeal and mundane experiences. It is not just an incorporeal specter.

Implicit in Christianity for Tertullian is an active appreciation of the body as a sacred entity. This is supported by the sacrament of the Eucharist and the assertion that the Word was made flesh

This assumption becomes a critical element in later Christian doctrine and stands as a barrier against reincarnation finding acceptance within

Christianity. For the present, Tertullian steers clear of the state of the soul between the time of death and the resurrection of the body. The soul's reflections about the post-mortem existence of friends and loved ones, however, does suggest pagan belief in their post-mortem existence.

Now, O soul, for something that impinges even more immediately on your awareness—how this reaches out to your very essence!—we are affirming that you survive beyond the final reckoning and that you can expect a day of judgment when you are eternally consigned to torment or delight according to your merits. In order to undergo this you must recover your original essence by reviving the substance and memory of the person you once were. Without the awareness of sentient flesh you can perceive neither good nor evil; there is no basis for judgment without the living presence of the one who actually earned the inflicted punishment. This Christian concept of the soul is more high-minded than Pythagoreanism, for it does not relocate you into animal bodies. It is more bountiful than Platonism, for it restores to you the gift of your very own body. It is more majestic than Epicureanism, for it delivers us from death. And yet solely because of the Christian name, this belief is rejected as a delusion or a misconception—or, as some say, an act of arrogant presumption.

By extending their expectations beyond the terminal expectations of the pagans, the Christians are engaging in what the pagans viewed as "an act of presumption." Tertullian does not make specific allusion here to the immortality of the soul in this treatise, but he comes very close in this passage. Without building a line of defense against the pagans, he alludes to the fact that the pagans had notions about the afterlife that transcended the term of mortal existence.

But we feel no shame for arrogant presumption, as this is a line of thought that we hold in common with you pagans. First, when you recall a deceased person to memory, you refer to him as "miserable," not because he has been snatched away from a good life but because he is condemned to punishment and judgment. At other times, however, we refer to the dead as "carefree," admitting that life is arduous and death is a boon. Moreover, you speak of them as "carefree" if you are venturing abroad to the tombs with dainty dishes and delicacies to entertain yourself in the name of the dead or if you are returning somewhat inebriated from cemetery festivities. But I am demanding your sober opinion. You refer to them as miserable when you are speaking from your present perspective, when you are at a distance from them. You really cannot find fault with the state of the dead when you are reclining and carousing as if in their actual presence. You have to extol those on whose account you are at the moment living festively.

Do you call him miserable who feels nothing? What about the one you curse as though he were aware? When someone has left you with the memory of a biting injury, you pray that the earth may rest heavy upon him and that his ashes suffer torment among the dead. By the same token, under benign conditions when you owe thanks, you pray that renewal may descend upon his bones and his ashes and that he may rest in peace among the dead. If after death there is in fact no awareness, no continuity of perception—if, in short, there is nothing left of you once you have left the body, why would you lie to yourself as if you could suffer any further? In fact, why do you fear death at all? There is nothing whatsoever to fear after death, for there is no experience after death.

As this section draws to its conclusion, Tertullian becomes arbitrary and irresolute. First, he writes about the possibility of an afterlife where the soul suffers the consequences of having offended a righteous and all-powerful God. Then Tertullian entertains the possibility that there is no experience at all after the end of life. There are moments in the flow of Tertullian's thought when he retreats from making unequivocal statements. The available resources were not conducive to such a stance.

He will now conclude this chapter with a final act of equivocation. When a pagan speaks about the possible return of the departed. He will

whisper under the shield of his hand the doctrine
of resurrection. Once again, Tertullian is claiming
that the soul may be irresolute, but its instinctive
awareness of Christian truth is a recurrent reality.

One could venture to say that death should
be feared, not because it threatens any further
hardship, but rather because it cuts off the
delights of life. But fear of death is diminished
by a much more significant dividend. The
hardships of life—far more numerous than the
delights—depart at the time of death. The loss
of pleasure is not to be feared when it is weighed
against another boon, namely the loss of hardship.
Nothing is to be feared that frees us from all fear.
If you fear to depart from life, which you know
as a supreme good, you certainly should not fear
death, which you do not necessarily know as evil.
But when you fear death it is because you know
it is evil. However, you would not know it as evil,
nor would you fear it, were it not for the fact that
there is something after death that renders it
evil—so that in fact you do fear it.

Let us now leave aside our instinctive fear
of death. Let no one fear what he cannot avoid.
Coming from a different perspective, I shall now
consider death as the source of happier hopes.
Almost everyone is endowed with an inborn
desire for fame after death. It would be overlong

to review Curtius and Regulus[1] and the Greek men about whom there are countless eulogies of their contempt for death in expectation of posthumous fame. Who today does not strive to celebrate his own memory after death so that he may preserve his name either in works of literature or by the recognition of his good character or by the grandeur of his tomb? Why is it that in the present the soul wishes to provide something for after death and fashion it with such exertion for use after passing? The soul would care nothing for the end unless it knew something of the end. Or perhaps you are more confident of consciousness after your passing than you are about resurrection—for which belief we are censured as being presumptuous. This too, however, is proclaimed by the soul. If anyone inquires about someone already dead as though he were alive, we answer from beneath the hand, "He has departed and he must come again." [2]

---

[1]   Curtius and Regulus were mythic heroes in Roman history.

[2]   Here Tertullian is exercising Christian caution and restraint when reflecting on the extreme post-mortem benefits of the new faith.

CHAPTER V

THE TEMPORAL PRIMACY OF THE SOUL

Tertullian now seeks to demonstrate why the testimony of the soul supersedes anything based on written evidence. This task is accomplished not so much by sequential argument as by direct assertion. Whatever the soul knows has been conveyed by nature and whatever nature knows has been conveyed by God. Intrinsic to the thought of Tertullian is that God pervades our surroundings in this world, and an operative term for that reality is *Natura*—Nature. The authority for this supposition is not stated; but the educated pagan might well accept it without further reflection because of its affinity with traditional Stoic thought. From here the argument flows with ease. Since the soul predates published works, philosophy, and writing, its teachings about God and the afterlife cannot be traced back to written words. They arise spontaneously from within—which is to say from God. It now follows that Christian thought has not made some kind of a presumptuous journey from its pagan origins. It is the natural expression of the "divinely-instructed" soul.

These testimonies of the soul are as true as they are straightforward, as straightforward as they are widespread, as widespread as they are universal, as universal as they are natural, and as natural as they are divine. I do not believe anyone would find it frivolous or laughable, if he reflects on the majesty of nature, which is regarded as the wellspring of the soul. As much as you attribute to the teacher, so much you will concede to the pupil. The teacher is nature and the pupil is the soul. Whatever the teacher has conveyed or the pupil has learned has been communicated by God who is the teacher of nature. Whatever the soul can surmise about its original teacher, this power resides in you that you pagans may reflect upon that which is in you. Be aware of that which has given you awareness. Recognize her who is the seer of your forebodings, who is the prophet of your inklings, who is the oracle of your outcomes. Is it any wonder if, having been bestowed by God, she holds divine powers prophecy? Is it any wonder if she knows God by whom she was bestowed?

Even when the soul is deceived by the adversary, she recalls her creator, his goodness, his decree, her own fall, and the fall of the adversary. Is it any wonder if, having been bestowed by God, she pronounces those things which God gave his creatures to know? But whoever does not think that these explanations of the soul are the promptings of nature and the silent expressions of our inborn and native awareness, he will attribute them to the vice of citing opinions from the published literature in circulation among the masses.

Certainly the soul predates writing, and speech predates the book, and thought predates the pen, and man himself predates the philosopher and the poet. Is it to be believed that before literature and its spread, man lived in silence on such subjects? Did no one ever speak of God and his goodness? Did no one speak of death and the afterlife? Speech, I believe, was impoverished, in fact nonexistent, if it once lacked those elements without which it cannot exist today. And now, of course, speech is richer, fuller, and wiser than ever before. If those things that today are so accessible, so immediate, so near at hand, so springing from the lips—if they did not exist before writing emerged, before, as I believe, Mercury[1] was born—then indeed speech was a beggar. How was it possible, I ask, that literature could know and embark into spoken usage, expressing what no mind had previously conceived, no tongue had uttered, no ear had heard?

But since the divine scriptures belonging to us or to the Jews—onto whose olive branch we have been grafted—who are much older or at

---

[1]   The god Mercury was credited with the invention of writing.

least somewhat older than pagan literature, then credence must be given to our literature rather than to yours. Our literature is more forceful for instructing the soul than yours, having come into being earlier rather than later. Even if we grant that the soul was educated by your literature, tradition derives from its primal origin. Whatever you have taken or assimilated from our letters is still ours. This being the case, it does not make a great deal of difference whether the awareness of the soul was shaped by God or by writings about God. Why, O humankind, why do you insist that these notions about the soul emerged from opinions about your writings, only to ripen then into common usage?

CHAPTER VI

TESTIMONY BEYOND LANGUAGE AND

CULTURE

This tract concludes on a triumphant crescendo. Tertullian says we are all joined by the common bond of our humanity which in turn is united by the testimony of the soul. The spontaneous utterances of the soul cut across language, culture, race, and time. The soul is a repository for these primal inklings because it has been instructed by Nature which had a distinct place in pagan philosophy. Having now proven that the soul is by nature Christian, Tertullian hopes that the pagans will be convinced that, by persecuting the Christians, they are in fact acting against their own deepest nature. This concluding chapter is a summons to the pagans to comply with the soul's natural penchant to expound Christian belief.

Go ahead and believe in your literary sources; even more believe in our divine sources. But as for the insight of the soul, believe in Nature. Select whichever of these you believe to be the faithful sister of the truth. If you have doubts as to your own sources, be assured that neither God nor Nature lie. In order that you may believe in both Nature and in God, believe in the soul. So it shall come to pass that you will believe in yourself. It is the soul you value as having made you as great as you are.

You belong to her entirely; she is everything to you. Without her you can neither live nor die. For her sake you neglect even God. When you fear to become a Christian come onto her. Why does the soul invoke the name of God when she is worshiping another? When she enlists spirits for cursing, why does she address them as demons? Why does she invoke the heavens and curse the earth? Why does she serve the Lord in one place and summon his vengeance in another place? How does she judge the dead? What words does she take from the Christians whom she wishes neither to see nor to hear? Why does she either communicate these expressions to us or keep them from us? Why has she either taught us or learned from us?

Be suspicious of such a convergence of words amidst such a divergence of the message. You are deluded if you attribute this to the Latin language alone or to the Greek language, which is closely related, for you are thus denying the universality of nature. The soul has descended from heaven, not just on the Romans and the Greeks. One humanity comprises all races, although the name varies. There is a single soul but language is various. There is a single spirit but speech is various. Every race has its own discourse but the content of this discourse is universal. God is everywhere and the goodness of God is everywhere. The demons are everywhere and the curse of the demons is everywhere. The summons of God's judgment is everywhere. The awareness of death is everywhere and the testimony of the soul is everywhere. By its own right every soul proclaims those things we Christians are not even allowed to murmur. Rightly then, every soul is both defendant and witness—as much a defendant against the charge of error as a witness to the truth. And she will stand before the court of God on the Day of Judgment with nothing to say. You were preaching God but you were not seeking him. You shuddered before the demons and still you worshipped them. You would invoke the judgment of God and yet you denied it. You believed in eternal punishment and yet you took no steps to avoid it. You were aware of the Christian name and yet you have persecuted it.

The chapter concludes with a radical and profound challenge. The pagans have been engaging in a wide and disparate range of reflection, judgment, assessment, and search for the truth. What is unique about Tertullian is that he has a mentality that is able to move back and forth with ease between spiritual affirmation and philosophic reflection. There is a fluidity of mental posture that presents Tertullian as a likely candidate for conversion to the new faith of Christianity. There is a will to believe and a notable degree of mental receptivity.

CONTENTS

To the Nations

CHAPTER 1

TO BE CONDEMNED IS TO BE BLESSED

The Latin title of this tract is *Ad Nationes*, whose literal meaning is To the Nations. The nations are those whose immediate and identifying allegiance is to the Roman state. This is a category that excludes Christians, which is the term for someone whose immediate and identifying allegiance is to the teachings of Christ. Tertullian lived at a time when Christians were being killed by pagans for their failure to accord their ultimate loyalty to the state. Under such conditions there is clearly going to be a radical division between pagans and Christians. To be a Christian is to take one's life in one's hands and run the risk of execution.

Some of the charges made against the Christians were indeed alarming: incest, infanticide, adultery, and cannibalism. Are these rumors true? The circumspect answer of Christian scholarship is probably not. There were a number of factors that contributed to this malicious gossip about the Christians. First, the Romans were surrounded by religious cults across the Empire that were notorious for savage practices—Druids, devotees of Bacchus, the Egyptians, the rites of Thyestes and

Oedipus. Second, the Christians conducted their worship in secrecy. This practice was associated with cults that had something to hide. Third, there were various Christian splinter groups that were remotely Christian, partially Christian, or just nominally Christian. And finally, the sacrament of the Eucharist—consuming the blood and flesh of your founder—may well have confounded the literalism of the pagan mind and suggested possible cannibalism. In the same vein the pagans may have been misled by the Christian emphasis on brotherly love and mistaken this as an easy door to incest.

A further item of lurid rumor about the Christians was that they would stage banquets illuminated by upright candleholders. As a signal to let the festivities begin, dogs bound to each other by a cord would be released and someone would toss a morsel of meat across the room. The dogs would then dash about, knocking over the lights. One may also legitimately ask what is the likelihood that believers who are willing to die for their faith would conduct their lives in such riotous misconduct.?

Throughout his writings Tertullian belabors the ignorant, prejudiced, and misinformed view of the pagans. He dwells on the inconsistency of their charges against the Christians and the harshness of their judgment. This opening chapter invites the pagan reader to rethink his prejudice against Christianity and take steps to mitigate the drastic measures being taken against this new dispensation.

The evidence for your ignorance is plain to see. As you defend your position, you refute it. Now touched by new insight, all of you who once were ignorant of Christianity and declared your hatred have put that hatred aside and are no longer ignorant. In fact you have become what you once hated and now hate what you once were.

Every day you groan over the proliferating number of Christians. You fret that the state is overrun by Christians—in the fields, on the barricades, on the islands. You mourn the fact that every sex, every age, and every social class is crossing over from you to us. Nor does it occur to you that something good might lie hidden here. You avoid straight thinking and you shun an open mind. Human curiosity lies fallow. You delight to ignore what others are thrilled to have discovered. As long as you hate you prefer to remain ignorant, fearing that once you know you will cease to hate. But if there is no merit to be found in your hatred, it is surely best to set aside your earlier injustice. On the other hand, if there has been just cause let there be no decline in your hatred because it is now all the more fortified by an awareness of justice. Unless, of course, you are ashamed to mend your ways or you are reluctant to clear your reputation.

I am well aware of how you choose to respond to the evidence of our growing numbers. You say that it is not necessarily a good thing that Christianity is winning over so many new converts. I am also aware of how the mind can take a turn toward evil. How many forsake the path of virtuous living? How many seek refuge in twisted ways? Very many is the answer—many indeed—considering the approaching end of time. But this trend of thought is defective. As far as evil is concerned, everyone agrees that, although there are those who seek evil and forsake goodness, not even such egregious culprits and malefactors would presume to defend evil in preference to the good.

They fear what is low-minded; they are ashamed of impiety; they yearn to hide; they shudder to be seen; they tremble when they are caught; they deny when accused. Not even under torture do they readily confess. At least they grieve when condemned; they loathe what they have become; and they blame fate for their journey from innocence to malice. They seek to divest themselves of the evil they cannot deny.

How do Christians deal with being condemned for their faith? None feel shame. None feel oppressed unless by the weight of earlier sins. When a Christian is pointed out, he rejoices. When apprehended, he submits. When accused, he makes no defense. When questioned, he confesses. When condemned, he rejoices. Can this reaction be called evil when the very nature of evil is being thwarted?

CHAPTER II

TO CONFESS IS TO BE BLESSED

Tertullian is always alert for paradox, and a recurrent theme in the *Ad Nationes* is the paradox of applying torture to the Christians so that they will confess their faith. Ordinarily a confession occurs when a suspect is forced to say something he does not wish to disclose. From the pagan perspective, to be a Christian is a crime. For the Christian, however, to confess his faith ensures the promise of eternal blessedness. The pagans torture the Christians to admit the one thing that is the emblem of their blessedness. Hence the judicial process of forcing a confession is absurd. One confesses to robbery or murder, but not to one's greatest treasure which is Christian belief.

In your treatment of us, you actually reverse the norms of judging criminals. When conventional offenders stand trial you will apply torture if they deny the charge. But when Christians make a spontaneous confession of their faith you will apply torture that they may retract their words. What perversity you indulge! You take up arms against the confession and reverse the role of torture. He who willingly confesses you force to evade his faith, while he who is already unwilling to confess is actually forced to deny the charge. You, the coercive guardians of the truth, constrain only the Christian to lie, forcing us to deny the very thing that defines us. In point of fact, I believe you do not wish to convict us as evil men; you actually wish to exempt us from that charge. Conversely, you torment and butcher non-Christians that they deny the charges against them. But when they deny the charge you do not believe them. In our case, however, you will believe us immediately if we will deny the charge of being Christian.

If you are not actually convinced that we Christians are the most menacing defendants, then why are we dealt with so differently from other defendants? When dealing with other defendants, you allow ample time for accusation and denial. You are, in fact, in the habit of readily condemning defendants without due process. In the instance of the murderer, for example, the case is not settled and the inquiry finished as soon as a defendant confesses. Even in the face of the confession, you entertain doubts and questions. You examine the aftermath, how often he has committed the same crime, what weapons were used. Why did it take place? What was the gain? Who were the accomplices? Who the beneficiaries? Every step is taken to ensure that nothing about the accused escapes notice, that nothing is lacking for determining the truth.

When dealing with us Christians, however, who have been found guilty of more vicious and more numerous crimes than homicide, you invoke shorter and more trivial charges. I suspect you do not wish to heap on the charges since you already intend to destroy us entirely. Or else you feel there is no need to research what you already know about us. It is even more perverse that you force us to deny what you have already ascertained about us, namely that we are Christians. It would be more in keeping with your hatred for us to put aside due process and stop straining to make us deny our faith. If we do deny our faith, then you would have to acquit us whom you hate.

How much more rewarding for your hatred of us to force confession one crime at a time and heap on the punishments one at a time. How many lewd banquets did each defendant attend? How many incestuous get-togethers under cover of darkness? Since your need to eradicate our kind is overflowing its banks, why not extend your investigations to our friends and fellow conspirators? Let's bring on the infanticides and the butchers and the conjugal canines who stand guard over our incestuous weddings. What a quick and convenient fix! Think how eagerly people would flock to the spectacles! Imagine how avidly they would converge to watch a combatant who had devoured a hundred infants!

If such chilling and monstrous charges are reported against us, they need to be brought to light. Otherwise they will seem incredible and the public hatred toward us could grow cold. Many people are reluctant to believe such things, assuming that nature prevents humankind from feeding and mating like wild animals.

CHAPTER III

ACCUSATIONS WITHOUT PROOF

This chapter continues to belabor the legal paradox of the Christian position. The only actual charge against the Christians is that they assent to the charge that they are Christians. There is no investigation into criminal activities. There is no attempt to adduce a direct connection between the specific defendant and the illegal rites of infanticide and incest that had become associated with Christianity in the pagan mind. It is not sound legal practice to prosecute a person merely for the Christian name.

You have been zealous and tenacious in prosecuting crimes far more trivial than ours, and yet for us you abandon your habitual diligence despite the savagery and towering outrage of your charges. You neither record a confession nor do you carry out an investigation—both essential aspects of a criminal proceeding. It is apparent that the sole charge against us consists not in some criminal act but in our name.

If this were a matter of a valid charge, the name of the charge would match the designation of the defendant. An accusation would be issued against "this murderer" or "that incest offender" or whatever charge fits. Then that defendant would be led off to be executed or crucified or fed to wild animals.

Your verdicts, however, have condemned nothing but a Christian confession against us. There is no name of a charge against us, just the charge of a name.

Herein lies the entire reasoning and substance of the hatred against us. The name alone is a crime. A certain insidious force assails you and is empowered by your ignorance so that you do not wish to know with certain knowledge that very thing of which you have certain ignorance. Thus you do not wish to know things that are not proven and, lest they be readily proven, you do not wish to make further inquiry to ensure that the hateful name continues to be punished under the mere presumption of a crime. Now, in order that we dissociate ourselves from that hateful name, we are forced to deny all charges. Upon denial we are set free from the past with full impunity. We are no longer committing murder nor incest because we have divested ourselves entirely of our Christian name.

But since this line of reasoning is to be explored later on in its own right, please account for this vicious assault on our name. What crime, what guilt, what charge do you attach to this name? You are constrained by your own legal code from presenting charges where there is no supporting ordinance, where no proof is adduced, where no sentence is declared. I acknowledge a legitimate plaintiff when the case comes before a judge, when there is a hearing, when there is a denial or confession, and when there is an adjudication.

But when it comes to the merit of a name—if a name faces charges or a word comes under accusation—I reject that a name or a word can give offense, unless of course the word sounds vulgar or implies bad luck or is degrading both for the speaker and the listener. Such words are to be condemned as crude, incorrect, or disgusting. The literal meaning of the word Christian, however, is an anointing. Even if you mispronounce the word as "chrestian"—you are not entirely clear about our name—your pronunciation suggests sweetness and goodness.[1]

You withhold from innocent men their innocent name, a name that is neither challenging to the tongue nor harsh to the ear nor offensive to any man, nor provocative to our peers. Like

---

[1]   The Greek word χρηστος (chrestos), erroneously associated at times by the pagans with Christian, means good or pleasant.

many Greek words, it is appealing in both sound and significance. Names were never meant to be punished by the sword, nor by the cross, nor by ravenous beasts.

CHAPTER IV

PAGAN CONDEMNATION OF

CHRISTIAN GOODNESS

When a man admits to being a Christian does he then give evidence of some punishable offense? The answer is clearly "no." The name Christian merely implies the name of the founder just as the Platonists are followers of Plato. And far from finding moral defects in those called Christians, we find that they generally exhibit qualities of moral excellence. So great is the pagan prejudice against Christianity that they will refuse to acknowledge or give credit for the change of character that generally accompanies Christian conversion. This is borne out by the bizarre and paradoxical account of a man who rejected his wife after she became a paragon of Christian goodness.

But you say this sect is being punished in the name of its founder. First of all, it is certainly legitimate and customary to name the sect after its founder. This naming is true of philosophers who are Pythagoreans or Platonists. Physicians are named Erasisistratus and grammarians are named after Aristarchus. If this Christian sect is found to be evil because of an evil founder, then it is being punished on the persistent strength of an evil name. But this would be an act of rash presumption. In order to understand a sect, first acquaint yourself with the founder rather than repress this whole line of inquiry.

When it comes to the Christians, however, you are of necessity ignorant of the sect because you are ignorant of the founder. Or you give no thought to the founder because you give no thought to the sect. In either case you fix on the name alone as if it gave you power over the sect and the founder. And you remain entirely ignorant of both.

And yet your philosophers are at liberty to cross over from one founder and name to another. No one provokes hatred against them even when they spew forth both open and veiled loathing for your customs, your rights, your ceremonies, and your entire style of life. With contempt for the law and respect for no one, the philosophers vaunt their wanton abuse even against the emperors.

But there is a truth, hateful to this world, which the philosopher's grab at and which the Christians possess. Those who possess this truth incur the greater wrath because those who grab merely dabble in it while those who possess it rise to its defense. Take the instance of Socrates—as he drew ever closer to the truth, he was condemned to death for denying the pagan gods. Even though at that time the Christian name was unknown to the world, the actual truth was always condemned.

You cannot deny that Socrates was wise when the Pythian Apollo said, "Socrates is the wisest of all men" (Plato, *Apology*, 21a). The truth so overpowered Apollo that he would declare even against himself, confessing that he was not a god and affirming that one who denied the gods was the wisest of men. By your account, Socrates is less wise because he denied the gods when in fact he proved his wisdom by denying them.

Just as you are accustomed to say of us, "Lucius Titus is a good man except for the fact that he is a Christian," someone else will say, "I am surprised that Gaius Seius, such a high-minded man, has become a Christian." Guided by their blind stupidity, men will praise what they know and condemn what they do not know. They will take what they know to tear down what they do not know.

It never occurs to anyone that a person is good and decent because he is a Christian or that he has become a Christian because he is good and decent. It is more in keeping with human nature to judge hidden attributes of what is evident than to condemn what is evident by hidden attributes. Some people wonder that those whom they had known to be lost, low-minded, and immoral before taking up the Christian name are suddenly transformed. But they know only how to marvel at this change and not how to achieve it. Then there are others who struggle with such stubbornness against their own welfare which they could advance by making common cause with the Christian name.

I know of one or another husband who was so anxious about his wife's morals prior to her conversion he would groan with apprehension if a mouse crept into the bedroom. Upon the conversion of the wife to Christianity, however, he bestows total conjugal liberty on her, realizing that her religion was the source of her new rigor and rectitude. He now denies any jealousy and insists he would rather be married to a she-wolf than to a Christian woman. He has taken the liberty of corrupting his own nature; but he forbids his wife to change for the better.

A father disinherited his son in whom he could find no fault. A master threw an invaluable slave into prison. As soon as you know someone is a Christian you wish to prove his depravity. Our moral code exposes who we are and we are betrayed by our own goodness. In like manner, evil men shed light on their own depravity. We alone, contrary to the conventions of nature, are singled out as depraved because of our goodness.

What do we raise on high as our distinguishing mark if not primal wisdom? We do not worship the works of the human hand. We exercise restraint in dealing with others. We do not compromise our sense of shame with a wanton glance. We offer compassion to the hard-pressed. We cultivate the truth though it gives offense. We have embraced liberty though it be the liberty to die. If you wish to know who the Christians are then these are the signs by which you may know us.

CHAPTER V

TO FALL SHORT OF THE CHRISTIAN NAME

Here Tertullian raises an interesting question to which there is no single, unequivocal answer. To what extent is the quality of the Christian faith to be judged by the behavior of those avowed believers who fall short? One can, of course, affirm that perfection is an unrealistic expectation. The most perfect blue sky will be tainted by the wisp of a cloud. A perfect complexion will show a freckle. One can recognize the fact that among avowed Christians there will always be those who do not meet the full measure of expectations. In like manner, there are self-declared philosophers who do not live up to all the name implies. When this occurs within the Christian community, those who fail to conform in full measure are in fact implicitly rejected. This stern verdict closes the chapter.

You charge that we are depraved and utterly corrupted by greed, luxury and immorality. We do not deny that this is true of some of us. It is, however, sufficient evidence of our good name if it is not true of all of us, not even true of most of us. It is true that even the purest and most pristine body is subject to the occasional intrusion of a mole, a wart, or a freckle. Not even the lustrous clarity of the sky remains untouched by the wisp of a passing cloud. A minute blemish on the brow, a conspicuous location, serves to proclaim the purity of the visage. A tiny spot of evil bears witness to the greater good of the whole.

When you demonstrate that some of our followers are evil, you do not thus prove that they are Christians. Search out any sect accused of evil. When in conversation about us, you say, "Why is this one a cheat if the Christians have such self-control? Why is that one so unfeeling if the Christians are so compassionate?" When you charge, "How can Christians behave in these vile ways?" You are in fact giving witness that this is not typical Christian behavior.

There is a great divide between a name and a crime, between an opinion and the truth. Names were created to draw a sharp line between actual existence and mere name-calling. How many people are called philosophers who have failed to live out the law of philosophy? All wear the name of what they profess, but if they bear that name without fulfilling the excellence of what they profess, they are defaming the truth with the artifice of speech. They do not suddenly become what they claim to be. And since they are not what they claim to be, the name is used in vain and they are deceiving those who attach substance to the name. The authority of the name is confirmed by compliance with the reality.

But people of this type neither congregate with us nor do they engage in worship with us. By their dereliction they fall back into your midst. Indeed we do not even mix with those who have been forced to recant by your violence and savagery. We would of course more gladly welcome into our midst those who have abandoned their faith under coercion over those who have done so willingly. Moreover, it is not legitimate for you to designate as Christians those whom the Christians themselves have denied. Such fallen ones do not even grasp their own denial.

CHAPTER VI

CONDEMNATION WITHOUT EVIDENCE

There is a further fallacy in the legal procedures by which the Christians are persecuted. They are charged with one or another of the vices associated with Christianity—adultery or infanticide—to name two. But the courts never conduct an investigation to determine whether such a crime has been committed. They will simply pronounce a verdict against a defendant, satisfied that the charge of being a Christian guarantees culpability of the habitual Christian vices. Not sound procedure!

Your conscience, silent witness of your ignorance, is chastened and coerced by our rejoinders, which are spontaneously suggested by the truth itself. Then you seek desperate refuge in the authority of the laws, which would not punish this sect unless there were a consensus among the founders of your laws as to the merits of this sect. Is there anything to prevent those who enforce the laws in similar cases from conducting a full investigation before passing sentence? In the instance of homicide or adultery, for example, the sequence of events is subject to full discussion, even though the exact nature of the crime is already known to all.

The pagan goal is simply punish the Christians without due process. Whatever crime the Christian has committed must be brought to light. There is no law to prevent an investigation. In fact an investigation functions in the interest of the law. How will you enforce the law if you pass over the very offense that the law forbids and fail to take account of the available evidence? No law can rely on its own account of its righteousness; but it does owe such an account to those from whom it demands obedience. Moreover, a law becomes suspect if it shows no tendency to prove itself.

Thus the laws against the Christians are rightly held to be worthy of respect and compliance, but only as long as no one knows what they punish. But once the truth is known, however, namely that these laws enforced their code with swords, crosses, and lions, they are vehemently rejected as supremely unjust. For an unjust law there is no respect. I believe, however, that you entertain doubts about the justice of some of your laws, since every day you issue new statutes and decrees to mitigate their brutal and wanton execution.

CHAPTER VII

REPORTS OF CHRISTIAN MISCONDUCT

ARISE FROM RUMOR

Tertullian now seeks the source of the reports of Christian misconduct. His answer to this is *fama*, the Latin word for rumor, a concept that was held in great ill repute by the Romans. Tertullian quotes a famous line from Virgil where rumor is reviled as being swift and malevolent. Moreover, it is by definition the bearer of false information.

Persecution of the Christians goes back to the time of Nero who was notorious for his character defects. And in 198 AD, 200 years after its origin, Christianity is still subject to persecution. Let us consider the reliability of these two Christian enemies—Nero and rumor. Tongue in cheek, Tertullian raises the question of whether Nero was just and pure. The response of Nero's contemporaries and historians ever after has been a resounding "no." As to the reliability of rumor, the question speaks for itself in the very definition of rumor.

Tertullian closes the chapter at the peak of his facetious talent, presenting the hapless candidate for Christian acceptance who has neither an infant available for sacrifice nor a mother or sister available for a sacred tumble in the dark. Is it remotely conceivable, he asks, that such depraved acts could be the rite of passage into the Christian faith? Or has rumor perhaps misled us?

You will say, how is it possible that such a hideous reputation has grown up around you Christians as to convince our lawmakers of its testimony? And I shall ask who was the advocate for your lawmakers in their own time and for you in the present time to vouch for this reputation? Could it perhaps have been:

Rumor, an evil of relentless speed (Aeneid IV. 176).

But why evil, if it is always true? Is it in fact not largely false? Even when it reports the truth it does not set aside its lust for lying. Rumor weaves falsehood in with the truth by a process of addition, subtraction and scrambling. She can maintain her existence only by lying. She lives on only as long as she fails to prove anything. As soon as a rumor is proven to be true, it expires.

Having conveyed its message, it departs. When the report is real and is declared a fact no one will say, "They say that this happened in Rome." Or, "Rumor has it that he has been assigned a province." Rather, it will be said, "This happened in Rome." Or "He has been assigned a province."

No one uses the term "rumor" unless he distrusts its truth. A rumor comes to nothing. Only conviction can become certitude. Only a fool believes a rumor because a wise man puts no trust in uncertainty.

Whatever the extent of its circulation, a rumor must derive its origin from a single mouth. Then from the conveyance of tongues and ears it creeps abroad, obscuring its original flaw as a rumor. As a consequence no one will recognize that a lying mouth first set it in motion, driven by a spiteful spirit or by a hint of suspicion or even by the sheer pleasure of lying.

But the good news is that time discloses all things, just as your opinions and proverbs testify—supported by nature herself. It is in the natural order that all things come to light, even those which Rumor never initiated. Consider what an extravagant Rumor you have enlisted against us. What it once proclaimed and has commended to the general attention now remains to this very day unproven.

Our Christian name first emerged when Augustus was emperor. During the reign of Tiberius, our beliefs shed their light abroad. Under Nero[1] condemnation flourished. You might give some thought to the actual character of our first persecutor. If he was just and chaste, then the Christians are immoral and wanton. If he was not an enemy of the people, then we are the enemy of the people. Our persecutor demonstrated our true character by punishing those who were at odds with him.

Of the movements from the time of Nero, only ours endures to this day—righteous in respect to our character and at variance with our persecutor. We have not yet been around for 200 years. By the report of Rumor there have been over this period so many perverse Christians, so many transfiguring crosses, so many infants slaughtered, so many loaves of bread soaked in blood, so many lamps extinguished, so many incestuous liaisons. And to date it is only Rumor that discriminates against the Christians.

Rumor gains its strength from the frailty of human nature and spins out its lies to the wanton and to the wicked. The more you incline toward evil, the more susceptible you are to

---

[1]   Nero was emperor from 54-68 and left a troubled legacy, which included the fire of Rome in 64 and then the persecution of the Christians as the supposed culprits behind the fire.

keep faith with evil. Then belief is more readily accorded to an evil lie than to a noble truth. If your injustice has left you with any capacity for discernment, then your sense of justice would demand that you assess the validity of Rumor. You would consider by whom such rumor was created and then advanced upon the people in general and to the world at large. I hardly think such condemndation was the work of Christians, since it is the nature and law of all religious mysteries that they be guarded by a vow of silence. And how much more would this be true of mysteries whose disclosure would incur swift condemnation thanks to general disapproval.

If we are not our own betrayers, then it follows that they are outsiders. But how would these purveyors of rumors gain knowledge of our mysteries, since even decent and lawful rites are guarded from public view? Unless of course they are even less contemptuous of illegal rites. But in fact outsiders are more inclined to be malicious rather than inventive when it comes to spreading rumors.

On the other hand, perhaps even our domestics were peeping through nooks and crannies to spy on us. What does it signify when even our domestics betray us to you? It would be better by far if no one were to betray us; but how much more fitting is it if our behavior is so vicious that the righteous rage of our domestics rips apart the good faith of the Christian household! They could not contain the affront to the mind and the shock to the eye. But it is even more extraordinary that the betrayer who leaps at the chance to report us is not concerned to offer proof while those who have heard these reports have no concern to see the evidence. This is assuming of course that the reward for the one who reports and proves his statement is equal to the reward for the one who hears it and convinces himself of the truth of what he hears reported.

By your account, first the deed is reported and then it is proven. First it is overheard, then it is examined. And then it is launched as a rumor. This surpasses all credibility. Here we have a charge that is detected just once but is confessed over and over again. The only plausible outcome is that we would have desisted from such practices entirely! And yet we are still called Christians and we still face the same charges and our numbers swell day by day. As we become more numerous the hatred grows. As the number of defendants thrives, why don't the informers thrive apace?

As far as I know, our practices have become better known. You now know the days of our meetings. We are now beset and beleaguered, forcibly detained in our own sacred meetings. But who has ever stumbled over a half devoured corpse at a meeting? Who has ever found tooth marks on a blood drenched crust of bread? Who caught sight of lewd behavior—let me not say incest—as a sudden shaft of light shot through the shadows? If we can offer a reward to prevent such offenses from coming under public scrutiny, then we can in fact prevent such disclosures entirely. Who will buy or sell the betrayal of a crime if it never existed in the first place?

But why should I lash out at these scouts and spies? You have charged us with offenses that you clearly have not heard us proclaiming with great fanfare. These charges have either been heard previously if they have already been brought to light or they are later made known if they had been previously kept secret.

No doubt it is the habit of those seeking initiation to approach the master of ceremonies or an elder who will say, "You must bring an infant, tender and wailing, to be offered as a sacrifice and you must bring a piece of bread to be broken and dipped in blood. Moreover, bring candle holders to be dragged around the room by dogs bound to one another. And then bring scraps of meat to incite these dogs. And of course be sure to bring along your mother or your sister."

But what if none of these necessities are available to you? I am afraid you are not going to make it as a legitimate Christian. Now I ask you, can such charges be launched by entire outsiders? It is obvious that they do not know what they are talking about. The first step in this process is launched by willful deceit. These banquets and incestuous nuptials are invented by totally ignorant informers. They have never even heard anything about the Christian mysteries. In time these informers will possess some actual knowledge to be passed on to others whom they bring along. But how absurd is it that these outsiders should know what is unknown to even the priest himself? Therefore they remain silent and carry about their information as accepted truth. They mention nothing by way of comparison from the tragedies of Thyestes and Oedipus.[1] They do not even draw attention to the ministers and masters of ceremony. And those who are well versed in the doctrine devour even more ravenous morsels during the ceremonies and without a sound. If none of this can be proven true, we have something of incalculable grandeur that confers upon us the strength to endure in the face of such atrocities.

O wretched and piteous heathens! Behold, we offer you the promise of our new dispensation. For those who follow it and persevere, it holds out the promise of eternal life. On the other hand, it threatens the profane and the contentious with the everlasting punishment of eternal fire.

For both the damned and the blessed there is resurrection of the dead.

But we shall deal with these beliefs later when they come under discussion. For the present, however, I urge you to believe in like manner with us. What I really want to know is whether you are prepared to advance in faith in the face of such crimes as you attribute to us. Come, whoever you may be, and bury your blade into an infant. Or is that someone else's job? Just gaze upon this expiring soul before it has ever lived. Gather in the raw blood, soak your bread, and dine with gusto. Then recline and check out the spot where your mother or your sister are bedded down. Take careful note so that when the shadows fall, relying on the precision of all parties, you do not inadvertently lay siege to some stranger. If you fail in your incest you will have to make an act of contrition.

Once you have performed this rite you shall live forever. Now let me ask you: is eternity really worth it? First of all, you do not believe this, and even if you did, you would be unwilling to pay this price. And even if you were willing, you would not have the vitality to do it. Why is it then that others can do this if you cannot? Why are you not able if others are able? What price would you attach to impunity and eternity? Can these be procured by us in any manner we choose? Does this mean

that Christians have a different set of teeth or
a different expanse of the jaw? When it comes
to incest, do they have a different perception of
pleasure? I hardly think so. It is sufficient for us
to part company from you on the strength of our
truth alone.

1.Thyestes had seduced the wife of his brother
Atreus, who staged a banquet of forgiveness. He
demonstrated his good will by serving a soup made
from the flesh of Thyestes' sons. Oedipus killed his
father and then married his mother.

This section ends in a rapid plunge into
outrageous logic. Tertullian endeavors to reconstruct
the train of thought that would enable a pagan critic
to engage in the Christian behaviors that have been
conveyed by Rumor. Is it then possible for an even
remotely normal human being to take an incestuous
tumble with this mother or his sister and then move
on with delightful anticipation to the joy of eternal
forgiveness?

CHAPTER VIII

THE HISTORICAL SEQUENCE OF NATIONS

There had been a recurring tendency in the early anti-Christian literature to refer to the Christians as a third division in humankind. The previous two were pagans and Jews. Here Tertullian takes on an absurd myth propagated by an early Egyptian king named Psammeticus (656 B.C.), who claimed to have determined the origin of human life in world. The story is primitive and silly, as Tertullian makes clear in his florid retelling of it.

The Dogface breed, mentioned in the second line of this chapter, occurs only once in Latin—right here. Dogface refers to anatomical irregularities mentioned in the last paragraph of the preceding chapter. The Shadowfoot class have huge feet so they could recline under the shadow of their feet while resting beneath the sun in the southern hemisphere. Anyone versed in drinking fresh blood and dining on human flesh would be a deviant version of the human species.

The thrust of the chapter, as Tertullian states at the end and elsewhere throughout his writings, is that any attempt to divide humanity into groups or races is meaningless. There is no nation that is not

Christian. Tertullian's unitive view of human nature is that humanity cannot be divided into distinctly various groups or races. The Christian essence is too pervasive. Human beings are in fact by nature Christian, which means that the pagan persecution of the Christians is an instance of humanity acting out of ignorance against its own nature.

It is said that we clearly belong to a third race of human beings. There are of course the Dogface breed, the Shadowfoot class, and the Antipodal freaks from the underside of the earth. If any of this makes any sense to you, I am begging you to tell us which is group one and which is group two so that we can agree on group three. Psammeticus thought that by the sheer force of his genius he had discovered a plausible theory of human origins. He is said to have isolated newborn infants from human contact and to have placed them in the care of a nurse whose tongue had been cut out. This step had been taken so that these infants would develop speech without any exposure to the sound of the human voice. Thus in speaking exclusively on their own initiative they would indicate what nation had first been prompted to speak. "Beccos," which is the Phrygian word for bread, is reported to have been their first utterance. Hence the Phrygians are the first race of humans.

But it would be relevant for me to point out this one fallacy of how you support your theories. I must observe that your position is supported not by verities but by vanities. Is it even remotely conceivable that this nurse could survive such an ordeal? Her tongue, that vital instrument of the soul, had been slashed out at the root. Her throat, a body part that can't even tolerate a superficial wound had been ripped open. And then, with gore running down her chest, she was deprived of food for extended time. Come now, she might have survived through the treatments of Philomela[1], whom wiser heads see as silenced by the blush of modesty rather than the removal of the tongue. But even if she did survive in this way, she would still be able to babble something—a dull and inarticulate sound or gurgling gasp—just by opening her mouth without even moving her lips, forced from her throat with her tongue now removed. This primal grunt, the only grunt available, the children perhaps practiced, but more skillfully since they still had their tongue. And then they gave it meaning.

So let's say that the Phrygians were the first race. The Christians still are not the third. How many successions of races came after the Phrygians? Just watch out that the race to whom you assign third place does not in fact claim the first place. There is indeed no race now that is not Christian. Whatever the first race was it is nevertheless now Christian. It is senseless insanity that you speak of us as the most recent race and then designate us as the third race.

But it is in connection with our beliefs, not our nationality, that we are assigned to the third position, as there are the Romans, the Jews, and then the Christians. And where are the Greeks in this? Of course if the Greeks are counted among the Romans, since Rome has been tampering with Greek gods, then where are the Egyptians? They stand apart, I believe, with an intricate religion. If we who occupy the third position are considered so abominable, what about those who came before us in positions one and two?

1. Philomela is the subject if several flamboyant mythic accounts. In *Tereas*, a lost play by Sophocles, Philomela is raped by Tereas, who is married to Philomela's sister Procne. In order to ensure Philomela's silence, Tereas cuts out her tongue. Philomela renders a visual account of her story in a piece of weaving which is conveyed to Tereas' wife Procne, who then takes revenge on Tereas by having his son Itys killed.

CHAPTER IX

THE GODS AS THE INSTRUMENT OF

DISASTERS

Inherent in pagan religion was a quick and causal association between the gods and bad luck. If there was an earthquake, a famine, a flood, it was because the gods had become irritated with human behavior and felt the need for punitive action. The pagans believed that their gods were especially irritated by the audacity of the Christians for not worshiping them. The pagan gods would retaliate by inflicting natural disasters, which were then viewed as punishment for Christian audacity.

This is an argument that abounds with absurdities and Tertullian points them out. First, numerous catastrophes occurred before the origin of the Christian dispensation. Second, the primary victims of these disasters had been pagans, the faithful devotees of the pagan gods. Third, many of these disasters took place before the pagan gods. Unlike the Christian God, who is without beginning or end, the pagan gods are fleeting players on the stage of history.

One of the major discrepancies between paganism and Christianity lies in the fact the Christian God and Christ both stand outside of time. This is a recurrent theme in scripture and was known to Tertullian. Consider the quotation, "Before Abraham was, I am." (John:8:58) One of the conceptual difficulties facing Tertullian as he tries to explain Christianity to pagan readers is the intrinsic transcendence of Christianity. For the pagan mind, even among the poets and philosophers, there was a fixity to time and space.

But why should I wonder at your mindless charges? Malice and folly, connected by a common bond, come into being under the single grandmaster of error. Since I am not in the least surprised at your charges, I feel constrained to enumerate them so that you may recognize your egregious stupidity when you blame us Christians for all public death and destruction. If the Tiber overflows, if the Nile recedes, if the heavens stand still, if the earth heaves, if some pestilence rages, if famine lays waste, you all cry out with a single voice: "It is the work of the Christians." As if those who do not fear God could have other petty fears.

By your account we provoke these disastrous dispatches from your gods because we hold them in contempt. As I mentioned previously, we have not even been around for 200 years. Prior to this think of how many disasters have fallen upon this world. Whole cities and provinces have perished. How many civil wars, how many wars of conquest? How many plagues, famines, conflagrations, heaving and cracking of the earth have the ages laid upon us?

Where were the Christians when Rome bore witness to such great travail? Where were the Christians when the islands of Hiera, Anaphe, Delos, Rhodes, and Cea sank to the bottom of the sea with many thousands of lost lives. And what of that great landmass, larger than Africa and Asia, that Plato claims to have sunk into the Atlantic Ocean?[1] And where were the Christians when fire from the sky struck down the Volusinii and flowed over the Pompeians from their own mountain?[2] Where were they when the Sea of Corinth burst open from an earthquake? Where were they when a flood devastated the whole Earth?

Where were your gods at this time? Forget about the Christians, the scorners of your gods! Your gods prove by the places and towns where they were born, where they tarried, where they were buried, and which they even founded that they came much later than these destructions. They would in fact no longer exist at all at the

---

[1]   Atlantis from Plato, Timaeus 24

[2]   Eruption of Mt. Vesuvius in 79

present time unless they came long after this original period of devastation.

If you don't even care to consider and contemplate the evidence of those times, recorded very differently by you, you will have to condemn your gods as unprincipled. They injure you their followers because of us their detractors. And then you prove yourselves to be mistaken if you keep faith with those gods who failed to distinguish you from the offenses of us profane Christians.

But if one or another fool has suggested that your gods are angry with you for not rushing ahead to destroy us, you have just proven their weakness and insignificance. They would not rage against you for being slow to chasten us if they could do it themselves. And yet you admit to this charge in other ways when you seek to avenge them by punishing us. If one party is to be avenged by another, the greater party delivers the vengeance. It is a disgrace when the gods must be defended by humankind!

CHAPTER X

THE VULGAR WORSHIP OF THE PAGANS

One of the most serious charges against the Christians was their contempt of the pagan gods. Tertullian suggests that if this is to be a pivot on which the persecution of Christianity turns, let us consider the quality of the piety offered by the pagans to their gods. He meets this challenge with glee. The pagans have betrayed the past and their own traditions. Because of the great number of gods, their followers are always favoring one while rejecting another. The worship is then regulated by the Senate, making it clear that the gods are subject to humanity rather than the opposite. The gods, their images, and their shrines are constantly serving commercial interests. Beyond this, when the gods are depicted in public spectacles, they possess the full range of human vices, to the great amusement of their worshipers. In short, the gods and their worship are managed by the whims and fancies of their pagan followers, while the Christians stand clear of them entirely.

Go ahead now and pour out your poison upon us. Let loose your arrows on this Christian name. I shall not desist from blocking them. Later on they will be blunted by the full disclosure of our beliefs. Now, however, I shall pluck these arrows from our own bodies and fling them back at you. I shall demonstrate that the same words of accusation are carved into your own bodies so that you may now fall upon your own swords and spears.

First, consider whether in fact you do not share with us the very charge you direct against us, namely that of abandoning the customs of the ancestors. When I consider the authority of your traditions and values, I find everything in wreckage and ruins. As for your laws, I have already pointed out that day by day you subvert them with new rules and regulations. When it comes to your general way of life, it is plainly apparent how much you have diverged from the ways of your ancestors. When it comes to conventions, personal style, attire, diet, even manner of speech, you are rejecting the past as though it were contaminated. The past has been entirely rejected in all of your practices and occupations. Present approval has entirely overruled the approval of your ancestors. It is all the more disgraceful that you praise the past and then persist in rejecting it. What perversity to have rejected the very customs that you now praise. These are the practices that should have prevailed among you.

The worship of the gods is the very tradition that you appear to guard and protect with the deepest good faith And this is a tradition in which you find us to be the most offensive culprits, the tradition from which the entire hatred of the Christian name derives its inspiration. But I shall now prove that it is you who are destroying and despising the worship of the gods.

There is no basis for charging us as despisers of the gods because no one can despise something that he knows does not exist. What exists can be the object of hate; what does not exist cannot be the object of anything. The gods can undergo suffering only at the hands of those who believe in them. You disgrace yourselves by believing and by sneering, by cultivating and offending, by honoring and by scoffing.

Here is a point to consider: some of you worship some gods and some of you worship others. And those whom you do not worship you hold in contempt. It is not possible to worship one without disregarding another. To accept one is to reject another. He who has embraced one from the many will despise one he did not embrace. Such a multitude of gods cannot be worshipped by everyone at once. Even at the very beginning you showed your contempt, unafraid to limit how many gods can be worshipped.

The most brilliant and discerning of your ancestors, whose traditions you are powerless to dismiss, betray themselves as impious. I am well aware of the fact that from time to time the pagans have decreed that a general must await approval from the Senate before he can dedicate a temple he promised to build in the event of victory. And yet Marcus Aemilius promised a temple to the god Alburnus without Senate approval. Is it not the height of impiety and insult that the honor of divinity is bestowed at the consent and concession of human opinion? There can be no god except at the pleasure of the Senate. Many times the censors have torn down a temple without consulting the people. They banished Father Bacchus and his rites not only from the city but throughout Italy. Furthermore Varro gives us an account of the ban from the Capital against Serapis, Isis, Harpocrates, and Anubis. Their altars, torn down by decree of the Senate, were restored by popular resistance. But on the following first of January, the Consul Gabinius grudgingly approved sacrifices to Serapis and Isis in response to popular agitation. Even though he had made no prior decision to support the decree of the Senate or to favor Serapis and Isis, he upheld the ban of the Senate, opposed the rush of the crowd, and forbade altars to be built.

Here among your ancestors you find, if not the name, then at least the practice of the Christians to neglect the gods. Even if you honor your gods, you are guilty of violating your religious norms. And I still find that you have advanced both in superstition and impiety. How you are declining in your religious observance! You retain your household gods, the Lares and Penates, by personal oath, and yet you trample them under foot, selling and pawning them to meet each passing whim. Such religious outrage would be more acceptable if it were not practiced with such measured moderation. There is, however, slight solace for the plight of your household gods only because you treat your public divinities even more wantonly and outrageously.

First of all, you offer your gods up for public auction. Every five years you put them up for sale among your other revenues. Thus you conduct business at the temple of Serapis and the temple of Jupiter. Then your gods themselves are brought in for barter at the bidding of the auctioneer, at the direction of the magistrate.

The fields have now become cheaper as they are encumbered by taxes. The very lives of men are devalued by capitation tax[1], for such are the

---

[1]   Taxation based on a "head count."

well-known penalties of servitude. But when it comes to the gods, the more tribute they generate, the more sacred they are and conversely, the more sacred they are the more tribute they generate. The majesty of the sacred is prostituted for profit. Religion itself is put up for sale. The sacred offers itself up for the highest bidder. You collect revenues from the temple grounds, from the entranceway, from the offertory, from the sacrifices. The divine itself is up for sale. Religion cannot be practiced free of charge. In the end the tax collectors are more bountifully recompensed than the priests themselves!

When it comes to your contempt, it was not a sufficient affront that you make the gods the objects of taxation. You were also pleased not just to withhold honor. Such honor as you do confer is debased by some form of outrage. Do you offer anything in their honor that you do not already confer upon your deceased in equal measure? You erect temples to your gods. You erect temples to your dead in equal measure. You build altars to your gods. The same for your dead. You confer the same titles on the gods as on the dead. You raise statues to them in the likeness of their talent, their occupation, or their age. Saturn appears as an old man. Apollo is clean-shaven. Diana is a virgin. Mars is a soldier and Vulcan is an iron smith. It is no wonder that you offer the same sacrifices to the divine and the dead and burn the same incense.

Who could excuse the outrage that you reckon any old dead person as equal to the gods? Indeed your kings are accorded the same sacred rites as the gods—grand vehicles to transport their statues, chariots, their likeness reclining on couches and chairs, wild beasts, and gladiatorial games. Of course since the heavens lie open to the kings, this is not without affront to the gods. First, it is indecent to reckon the kings as equal to the gods, as if it were granted to the kings to become gods upon their death. Second, any bystander who has seen a king received into the heavens would not explicitly and openly perjure himself before the people unless he had contempt both for his own oath and for those who permit him to lie.

Those who tell these lies have acknowledged that they are avowing nothing. Beyond that, they will pay off anyone who has openly scorned the penalties of perjury. In addition how many of you are free of perjury? Any danger from swearing by the gods has now vanished. There is now far greater religious fear in swearing by Caesar, which only serves to further diminish your gods. Punishment is more readily exacted for a false oath to Caesar than to Jove.

Between contempt and mockery, contempt is more honorable because it embodies a certain edge of pride. It arises from confidence, a clear conscience, and a natural elevation of the spirit. Mockery is more insolent and adds the bite of outrage. Notice how much mockery you offer to your gods. I won't even mention your sacrifices. You slaughter whatever is weary and wasted. From your robust and healthy animals you offer up what is nutritionally worthless—the head, the hoofs, the feathers, and the yanked out bristles. This is what you would toss into the garbage at home.

I shall say nothing of the disgusting gluttonous appetite that fed the religious practices of your ancestors. The fact is that the most learned and solemn of your ancestors—assuming that solemnity and wisdom are the product of education—were also the most irreverent toward the gods. Their literature never stopped proposing insulting, degrading, or false notions about the gods.

Let me start with your beloved poet. The more you honor him, the more you degrade your gods simply by exalting him who has made a mockery of your gods. I am referring of course to Homer, who has subordinated the majesty of the gods to the human condition. He inflicts upon them the faults and foibles of mankind. He depicts them in the various vicissitudes of gladiatorial combat. He wounds Venus with a human arrow. He detains Mars for thirteen months, perhaps to the very verge of death. He presents Jupiter almost expelled from heaven by a rowdy throng. Either he has Jupiter shedding tears over Sarpedon or presents him wantonly languishing for Juno. Homer further endorses Jupiter's passion by enumerating his sexual conquests. Since that time, who of the poets has not followed Homer's lead in insulting the gods, either by falsifying the truth or by making up lies? The tragedians and the comic writers have been no less offensive, proclaiming the hardships and punishments inflicted upon a god.

Let me be silent about the philosophers. Proud of their solemnity and austere in their doctrine, they are opposed to the gods. They are free of all fear and are guided by intimations of truth. Just to show his contempt for the gods, Socrates would swear by an oak tree or a dog or a goat. Even though he had been condemned to death, the Athenians repented of their sentence and meted out the same punishment to his accusers. The testimony of Socrates was vindicated and I can now retort that the contempt for the gods that was endorsed by him is now forbidden to us. There is Diogenes, who hurled some insult at Hercules and there is Varro, a Roman version of Diogenes, who introduced 300 Jupiters, all of them headless.

There are many lewd talents who tickle your fancy by degrading the gods. Consider the charming sacrilege of Lentulus and Hostius. Is it the performers or the gods themselves that you laugh at in their verses and jokes? You attend stage performances with the greatest glee where every filth of the gods is on display. The grandeur of the gods is represented by a lascivious body. The likeness of some god adorns the midget head of a notorious actor. To your delight the Sun mourns the death of his own son Apollo, struck by lightning. Cybele pants for a squeamish shepherd and you don't even blush. And you put up with Jupiter's jovial ditties.

When it comes to the gladiatorial shows you are even more devout. Condemned criminals are dressed up as gods and then your gods dance about through the blood and gore as convicts act out the plots and fables. We have often seen a criminal dressed as your god Attis from Pessinum undergo public castration. And we have seen someone burned alive while dressed as Hercules. We have laughed over the midday games of your gods when Father Pluto, brother of Jove, hauls off the remains of the gladiators brandishing his hammer or when Mercury wearing his winged cap and carrying his staff with tip smoldering, prods the dead bodies to see whether they are just playing dead. Who could even keep track of all these instances when they are degrading the honor of the gods and desecrating their majesty? This is contempt for the gods both on the part of those who produce these shows and those who actually participate.

For this reason I don't know if your gods should complain more about you than about us. On the one hand you cringe before them and on the other hand you pay them off when you fall short. In the end, you are at entire liberty to act toward them as you please. We, however, avoid them entirely.

Tertullian is a type of writer that is not a recurrent phenomenon in classical antiquity: he is running ahead of the vocabulary currently available. He was the first writer to use the word *"trinitas."* The word he is looking for in this essay is polytheist and he is running 1400 years ahead of time. It was first used in French in 1638. The somber reality is that paganism is not at ease with its own polytheism. This becomes vividly apparent when a monotheist like Tertullian comes face to face with paganism in 198 AD.

CHAPTER XI

ANIMAL WORSHIP AMONG

PAGANS AND CHRISTIANS

There was a tradition of Christian reverence for the head of a donkey and Tertullian treats it with levity in this chapter. Two earlier historians, Josephus and Tacitus, reported that the Jewish people, when lost in the wilderness, were delivered from thirst by a pack of wild asses that led them to drinking water. As a consequence, the Jews had attributed divinity to the head of an ass. This chapter makes frivolous play of the charge that the Christians, due to their kinship with the Jews, had also taken up the worship of the head of an ass.

As is often his practice, rather than refute the charge, Tertullian accuses the pagans of being even more egregious offenders. How can the pagans fault the Christians for worshiping the head of an ass when the pagans worship all kinds of animals from head to tail?

In the next accusation, we are found guilty not just of abandoning our communal faith, but of adding on a monstrosity of superstition. Some of you have entertained the dream that our god is actually the head of an ass. Cornelius Tacitus first launched this fantasy in the fourth book of his *Histories* where he recounts the Jewish war. Starting with the origins of the Jewish people, he traces the source of their religion and its name. He relates how the Jewish people, hard-pressed for water and wandering abroad in desolate places, were delivered by following the lead of a herd of wild asses thought to be in search of water after feeding. The likeness of this animal is worshiped by the Jew, and this is why I believe that we Christians, being linked to the Jewish religion, are associated with the same image. But the same Cornelius Tacitus, a runaway liar, forgetful of his earlier statement, relates how Pompey the Great, after defeating the Jews and conquering the city of Jerusalem, entered the temple. After close inspection he found no image whatsoever. Where was this god of theirs?[1] There was no more likely place than this remarkable temple, closed to all except the priests and secure against any outsider.

But what defense do you want from me? I'm admitting now to an occasional transgression that

---

[1]   Like chapter 4 on post-mortem existence, this chapter illustrates a common trait between Christianity and Judaism, namely a level of spirituality that transcends physical existence.

applies equally well to you. Let us suppose that that there is something asinine about our God. You certainly will not deny that you conduct the same worship we do. You, in fact, worship the ass in its entirety, not just the head. And then you throw in Epona, the patron saint of donkeys and all the beasts of burden, cattle, and wild animals. You even worship their stables. Perhaps this is your charge against us that in the midst of all these indiscriminate animal lovers we save our devotion for asses alone!

CHAPTER XII

WORSHIP OF THE CROSS: PAGAN AND

CHRISTIAN

Here Tertullian addresses the charge against the Christians that they worship the cross. By the time of Tertullian, the cross was a symbol of Christian redemption, so he feels no need to refute the charge. The reader will discover in this chapter, as is often the case, that the pagans have more in common with the Christians than they realize.

Taking the cross as a prototype of all pagan statuary, Tertullian argues that whether they know it or not the pagans also worship a cross. Whatever the intended subject and whatever the intended final material, the artisan starts with a wooden cross. He then forms clay around the initial structure and finally consummates his work in bronze or marble. But whatever the outcome, the primal form was a wooden cross. As in Chapter VIII, where Tertullian takes on the charge that the Christians comprise a third species of humankind, he finds here that the Christians constitute a temperate and pious instance of what is practiced by one and all.

He who calls us devotees of the cross shall be our fellow devotee. In its essence the cross is a wooden symbol. You also worship an image of wood, but for you that wood represents the human form, while for us the wood speaks for itself. Forget about the actual shape as long as the essence is wood; same for the form as long as the wood represents the form of a god. But if a distinction is to be made, what is the difference between a wooden cross on the one hand and a shapeless wooden strip representing Pallas Athena or Pharian Ceres on the other hand? Any piece of wood planted upright in the ground is part of a cross and indeed the larger part of a cross. But we Christians are credited with an entire cross complete with a transverse beam and a projecting seat.[1] You are all the more to be condemned because you present a deformed and rough-hewn chunk of wood while others consecrate a full and finished offering.

The fact of the matter is that in the end the fullness of your religion derives from the fullness of a cross, as I shall now show. You are not even aware of the fact that the very origins of your gods derive from the cross, this instrument of torment.

---

[1] The Romans would place a wooden ledge at waist level *(sedile)*, not as a gesture of kindness, but to prolong life. It was generally agreed that death by crucifixion was due to suffocation. The victim suspended at the hands would soon lack the strength to lift the rib cage and inhale. Thus, a small bench at waist level prolongs life.

Every image, whether it has been shaped from wood or stone, forged from brass or finished from some opulent substance, its shape was imparted by manual craftsmanship. Those formative hands first shaped the wood in the figure of a cross. This is because the very structure of our body suggests the essential and primal outline of a cross. The head ascends to the peak, the spine stands upright, and the shoulders traverse the spine. If you position a man with his arms outstretched, you shall have created the image of a cross.

With this cross as a starting point, the craftsman gradually fills out the limbs by laying on clay. By adding further layers of clay, he fills out the cross within to assume the body and posture of his original intention. Then, through the further refinement of precise drawing instruments and body parts cast from lead, the artisan transforms the cross into the likeness of a god fashioned of marble or clay or bronze or silver or whatever material suits his purpose. From the cross to the clay; from the clay to the god. In a manner of speaking, the cross becomes a god through the medium of the clay. You therefore consecrate the cross from which your consecrated god derives its origin. Indeed from the pit of an olive, from the stone of a peach, from the grain of a pepper plant—all of these—once placed beneath the soil, there emerges a full tree with branches and foliage true in every particular to its species. Now if you transplant it or start a new tree from a cutting, what would be the true origin of this transfer if not the self-same pit, stone, or grain? The third stage derives from the second and the second derives from the first and so the third stage takes its origin from the first through the intermediary of the second.

There is no further need to deliberate on this matter since the law of nature ordains that every species derives its type from its source. To the extent that the type derives from its origin, the origin is in accord with the type. If then you worship the cross as the origin of your gods, this will be the primal seed and source from which your wooden images are engendered.

Now for some examples. You revere your victories as gods, and the more grand the occasion, the more joyous the festivities. To heighten the sanctity of the occasion, crosses are the very guts and innards on which to display the trophies you have won in combat. In this way, the religion of warfare worships the cross in the ritual of victory. It adores these symbols, it swears vows by these symbols, it holds these symbols in higher regard than Jupiter himself. But this heap of images and this fetish for gold are no more than trinkets to decorate your crosses. The same is true of the banners and flags that your soldiers guard with no less veneration. These are simply petticoats for the crosses. I suppose you are ashamed to worship a plain and unadorned cross.

CHAPTER XIII

THE SUN AND SUNDAY

Tertullian now turns to the pagan charge that the Christians worship the sun and conduct their main worship service on Sunday. Once again, there are similar trends in pagan practice. The pagans, who disapprove of deviating from one's own ways, should acknowledge that in fact they have borrowed this inclination in favor of the Sabbath from the Jews.[1] Pagans and Christians again stand under the same condemnation.

Others of kinder disposition imagine that the sun is the Christian god. They have observed that when we pray we face to the east and we rejoice on the day of the sun. Do you do anything less than this? Do you not sometimes cause your lips to quiver toward the rising sun as an act of adoration? It is most definitely your preference to single out Sunday, the seventh day from the

---

[1]   It was generally agreed that the Jews and the Christians conducted their worship on the Sabbath and Sunday.

sequence, to refrain from bathing, at least until evening. This is also your designated day for leisure and festivity. By doing this you depart from your traditional practices in favor of alien religions. The Jewish festivals are the Sabbath and the feast of purification. And the Jews also have the rite of the lamps and of fasting with unleavened bread and prayers at the seashore, all of which are alien to your gods. Now to return to our subject, you who deride us for sun worship and Sunday worship, see how close you are to us. We are not far removed from your Saturn and your Sabbath.

CHAPTER XIV

THE "DONKEY PRIEST"

Although this chapter, like Chapter XI, deals with Jewish cult influence on early Christianity, Tertullian makes no connection. In Chapter XI he had defended the Christians against the charge that they worship the head of an ass. In this chapter he defends the Christians against the charge of venerating Onokoithes, a figure wearing donkey ears, clad in a toga, carrying a book, and wearing a hoof in place of the shoe on one foot. As with the earlier accusation, Tertullian does not deny the charge. He simply finds that the pagans commit the same offense and, as usual, to a greater degree.

There is now a new rumor about our God going the rounds. Recently a most depraved individual from Rome, your city, had defected from his own faith and allowed his skin to be shredded by wild beasts. Every day he would hire himself out for viewing while his skin was stripped. He would carry around a picture directed against us with the heading "Onokoithes," meaning Donkey

Priest. It was a picture of a man wearing a toga and the ears of the donkey with a book in hand and one leg ending in a hoof. And the crowd believed this Jewish man. Who else plants the seed of our infamous reputation? As a result the whole city is talking about the Donkey Priest. Since this rumor has been around since yesterday, it lacks any authority of time and is compromised by the character of its author. I shall now gladly use it to refute your charges.

Let us have a look if you are caught up with us in the same folly. If the image we cherish is a freak, it doesn't really matter what kind of freak. You have gods with the head of a dog, the head a lion, the horns of a cow, a ram, or a horny-headed goat. You have goat-form gods, snake-form gods, gods with winged feet, not to mention wings growing out of the brow and out of the back. Many a donkey priest is lurking in your midst.

CHAPTER XV

INFANTICIDE

Again we encounter the charge of infanticide and, like Chapter VII on Rumor, this chapter does not take the charge seriously. Tertullian merely observes that the pagans have a grotesque and cruel record when it comes to infanticide. They kill their own children and do so by exposing them to the elements, to wild animals, and to drowning. This killing is done not as a ritual sacrifice but as a means of population control. According to online sources, early Christianity was seriously resistant to infanticide. "Although ancient and pagan Greek and Rome had practiced and encouraged infanticide for hundreds and hundreds of years, Christianity fundamentally altered those societies. Christianity eliminated the promotion and encouragement of infanticide by government and leading societal institutions in Western Civilization. Clearly, one unique and valuable contribution of Christianity to Western Civilization was its opposition to infanticide." *Pagans, Christianity, and Infanticide*, Christopher Price. {2004)

If we are running on a parallel track with you pagans in respect to our gods, it follows that there is no real difference in respect to sacrifices and rites. Let us now look at a comparison of a different kind. You say we conduct our services and initiations with infanticide. In case your recollection of human sacrifice and infanticide is fading, it will be refreshed when the time comes. Let us postpone the main part of this topic for the present lest we seem to be treating the same subject all over the place.

Meanwhile, as I have said, there is another area of correspondence between us. We may be infanticides in one sense of the term, but you are infanticides in a very different sense. You are indeed forbidden by law from slaughtering newborn infants, but there is no law that is defied with such impunity and with such abandon, so publicly and with the legal sanction of all. But there is no real difference between us even if you do not kill infants as a sacred rite or with an iron blade. Your method is much more cruel because you expose the infants and kill them by frost, hunger, or wild beasts. Or you drown them by slow immersion in water. And if there is to be a further distinction between us, you can add the fact that you are exterminating your own beloved offspring. This aggravates and compounds whatever cruelty may be lacking on other grounds.

Moreover, we are said to dine on the victims of our sacrilege. While there is evidence of this in your practice, we can examine this charge at a more opportune time. We do have one thing in common with your savage appetite. If your vice is wantonness, then ours is cruelty, and we are joined by the law of nature, which always ordains a common bond between wantonness and cruelty.

Is there any outrage that you commit less than we do? In fact, what do you not commit more than we do? Are human innards too small a portion for you, you who devour full-grown living adults? Is it too small a portion for you to lap up human blood, you who draw out the blood of those yet to be born? Is dining on an infant too small, you who consume an entire infant as yet unborn?

CHAPTER XVI

AN INCESTUOUS TRAGEDY

We return now to the charge of incest and the egregious sinners to be found among the pagans. Tertullian recounts the brazen delight that Macedonian men take in sexual congress with their mothers and tells of the somewhat rowdy reception that *Oedipus Rex* receives when performed before a Macedonian audience. He then gives artful and loving attention to the recent scandal of a Roman boy of noble birth who strays from his home, is kidnapped, and returns to Rome and the slave market as a ripe adolescent. His father buys him and, not knowing his identity, uses him for sexual pleasure. The truth gradually emerges and the story comes to a grim conclusion. These pagans are indeed incorrigible!

We have now come to the hour of the lamps, lamp-dowsing dogs, and the diversions of the dark. Here I am afraid I may have to concede the greater restraint to you. What equivalent mischief can I charge against you? Do give us credit for our "chaste incest plan." We have contrived a counterfeit night lest we contaminate the light of day or the true gloom of night. We have seen fit to spare the light of day and so beguile our conscience. Whatever we do, we are able to blame ourselves if we feel the need.

Your incestuous acts, on the other hand, are committed with entire immunity in the light of day, in the fullness of the night, with the vault of the sky as your witness. And the outcome is all the more enjoyable because your incest is committed out in the open with the whole heavens looking on. You alone are unaware of what you were doing. We, however, do not deceive ourselves and hence can recognize our misdeeds, even in the dark shadows.

The Persians, as we know from the account of Ctesias,[1] fool around with their mothers with the full awareness and no regrets. The Macedonians do the same thing openly and with unreserved approval. When Oedipus first entered the Macedonian stage after putting out his eyes, they received him with jeers and sneers. The actor, drawing aside his mask in alarm said, "My lords, have I displeased you?"

"You have played your part beautifully," answered the Macedonians. They went on to say, "But either the author was a fool or Oedipus

---

[1] An obscure Greek historian of the 5th century whose work exists only in fragmentary form.

was demented to inflict such punishment on himself for mere incest." Then each Macedonian said to the person next to him, "He lay with his mother!!"

Does one or another individual contaminate the whole world? But you are claiming that we have contaminated the sun itself and have polluted the whole ocean. Show me one nation that is free from those images that entice the entire human race toward incest. If there is a single nation that is not subject to the sexual realities of age and gender, not to mention lust and luxury, that nation will also be free of incest. If there is a state of nature that stands aloof from the human condition, driven neither by ignorance, nor error, nor hardship, that alone will be able to respond unshaken before the Christians.

Consider the wanton ways that are riding the crest between folly and the winds. Is there a people whom this broad and harsh current does not dash against the rocks of incest? In the first place, when you offer up your children to the mercy of others or for adoption in hope of obtaining better parents, you forget what an opportunity for incest opens up, what a window for disaster. Clearly there are those among you who are reserved and restrain your lust from adventures of this sort. Whether at home or out of town, there's no reckless discharge of seed or lusty leap of exuberance to engender sons on unwitting recipients. Such progeny may then experience chance encounters in later life with their own parents or siblings. And then the restraint of maturity is powerless against the onslaught of lust. As often as there are adulteries or acts of debauchery or prostitution, whether at home or on the street, so many are the mixed strains of blood, so many are the joinings of family strains, and so many are the shortcuts to incest. It is from this stream that the plots of farces and low comedies flow forth. It was also from such a mess that the tragedy recently adjudicated by the prefect Fuscianus burst upon the city.

A young boy of noble birth had wandered away from his front door while his attendants were not watching. Enticed by some passersby, he slipped away from his home. He had a Greek tutor who had reared him from the outset and instructed him in the ways of pederasty. When the young boy came of age, he was brought back to Rome to enter the slave market. His father, unaware of who he is, buys him and uses him for sex. Then, after the boy had relations with the mistress of the family, the master sent him to the fields bound in chains. Both the tutor and the nurse had already been in the fields for some time and are undergoing punishment. The entire earlier course of events comes back to them and they recount the story of their departure. The tutor and nurse tell how their charge had died as a child, and the young man tells how his boyhood had been cut short. From this point, the stories converge. The young man had been born in Rome of a noble home. Perhaps he dropped some further hints.

And so it happened by the will of God that such a dreadful curse has fallen upon this age. All three of them are shaken in spirit on this day. The passage of time matches his age. There is something familiar about his glance and his profile. Some characteristic marks on his body catch their attention. His owners, now clearly his parents, launch a long overdue inquiry. The slave dealer is interrogated. Fortunately they had been able to find him. Once the crime is fully disclosed, the parents seek relief by hanging themselves. The prefect assigns their worldly goods to their son, a wretched survivor, not as an inheritance but as restitution for sexual defilement and incest.

This one incident was a sufficient example to expose the kind of outrage that lurks in your midst. Nothing occurs just once among the affairs of man, but for an incident like this, it is enough to bring it to light just once. I believe you are looking around for such scandals in the sacraments of our religion and yet there are equal outrages in your lives, quite apart from your religious practices.

CHAPTER XVII

THE DIVINITY OF THE EMPEROR

The failure of the Christians to swear by the divinity of the Emperor was a serious charge which could be construed as treason. And the Christians, in their belief in Christ as Lord, would often choose death rather than swear an oath to the divinity of Caesar. It emerges, of course, that the pagans are even more rebellious toward the emperors than the Christians, who have no history of revolt against Roman rule. Tertullian concludes this chapter with a witty turn of thought. To call Caesar God is to call him what he is not. If he had any choice in the matter, no doubt he would prefer to be alive as a high-stepping Imperator in preference to a rigidly grandiose pagan god.

Even in your complaints about our contemptuous resistance there are points of similarity between us. Our first act of contempt is toward the majesty of the Caesars who are second only to the gods. We are deemed blasphemous toward the Caesars because we neither worship their images nor do we swear by their divine spirit. We are defamed as enemies of the people. Well, so be it. First, realize that the Caesars name themselves after the enemies they have defeated in battle. There is Parthenicus, Medicus, and Germanicus. By using this nomenclature, the Romans name their emperor after the unconquered and far-flung nations of the world.

You also say against us, "The pagans and the Christians are of the same stock and yet you conspire against us." We acknowledge the Roman fealty to the Caesars. Indeed never has a conspiracy from us Christians broken out against the Caesars. No staining of the Caesars blood has ever defiled us, not in the Senate, not in the palace. Never have we usurped Roman sovereignty in the provinces.

The air in Syria is still heavy with the stench of cadavers. The Gauls still refuse to bathe in the Rhône.[1] I shall say nothing of your charge that we are insane since that does not contaminate the name of Rome. I shall, however, mention your charge of our boastful irreverence and I shall take note of the irreverence of your native-born proletariat and the outrageous handbills stuck to the statues, the insolent outcry at public assemblies, the curses that resound throughout

---

[1]   This event refers to the defeat of Albinus in March of 197.

the circuses. Even if you are not rebels in arms, you are always revolting in your speech.

But to refuse to swear by the divinity of Caesar is something else again. Even in the matter of perjury, you are open to suspicion since you do not even swear by your own gods with the conviction of faith. We do not say that the emperor is God. When it comes to this, we just make a monkey face as they say on the street. The fact is that those of you who call the emperor "god" are mocking him by calling him what he is not. And you are invoking bad luck because he has no wish to be what you are calling him. He would rather be counted among the living than become a god.

CHAPTER XVIII

HEROIC CONTEMPT FOR DEATH

The Christians were famous and much admired for their unswerving fortitude in the face of death. Although the pagans had many instances of heroic resistance in their history, they would accuse the Christians of stubbornness. Tertullian proceeds to cite outstanding instances of pagan heroism in the face of death. The problem here is really one of contradictory terminology. What the pagans hold to be glorious in their own practices they condemn as vanity and stubbornness in the case of a Christian.

Your remaining charge of contempt states that thanks to our austerity and our defiance of death, we gladly embrace the sword, the cross, wild beasts, fire, and torture. The fact is, however, that your forbearers and ancestors not only accepted such torments but, thanks to their courage, they learned to appreciate them with great praise. How many swords were there and how many willing victims? And what a pain to keep count! Your Regulus gladly introduced crucifixion as the novel instrument of numerous unreported deaths. And then there was the queen of Egypt[1] who did herself in with her personal snake. Inspired by the example of Dido, the Carthaginian wife of Hasdrubal, stronger than her husband in the death throes of their country, chose death by marching into a fire. Consider that Athenian woman who defied the tyrant and stood up to his torture. Lest her body and her gender fail her, she bit off her tongue and spat it out—the instrument of confession now uprooted. You credit such acts to your glory but discredit them to our stubbornness. Abolish the glory of your ancestors so that you may abolish our glory with the same reasoning. Be content to diminish the praise of your ancestors lest you confer praise on us for the same achievements.

Perhaps the demands of a more rigorous age required more rigorous character. But now, thanks to the tranquility of a peaceful age, character is more gentle and the minds of men are more compassionate, even toward strangers.

"Fine," you will say, "compare yourselves to the days of old. We still have to pursue you with hatred because of qualities we neither esteem nor possess." Respond then to these specific points.

---

[1] By popular account Cleopatra killed herself by taking a poisonous snake to her throat in 30 BC.

Do I not find the same behaviors in you? If the sword has given rise to stories about contempt for death, is it not out of love for life that you commit yourselves to gladiatorial trainers, sword in hand. Nor do you enlist in the military out of fear of death. Even if some woman once experienced an illustrious death from a wild beast, you do not run off to offer yourselves to wild animals, day after day and in this season of peace. Even if no next new Regulus has offered himself to a cross as the instrument of affixing his body, it was contempt for fire that recently compelled someone to hire himself out to proceed to a predetermined place clad in a flaming tunic. If a woman once danced to lashes from a whip, the same feat was recently performed by someone who recently paced out a fixed course through circus hunters under blows from a whip. No need to mention here the Spartan whipping spectacle.[2]

---

[2] The Spartans were famous for whipping their own children at the altar of Artemis. The parents would watch with pride as long as there was no painful reaction. See Tertullian, *Apologia*, L, 6.

CHAPTER XIX

HEAVEN AND HELL: PAGAN AND CHRISTIAN

Here Tertullian takes up what is probably the most treasured article of his Christian faith: the resurrection of the dead. Now he has no hesitancy with being both assertive and obstinate. Ultimately the vicissitudes of this world cannot touch the Christian because he will enjoy eternal blessedness when he departs this world. Once again, the possible folly of Christian belief retreats before the manifest absurdity of pagan beliefs about the afterlife. While the pagans believe in the resurrection of the dead, it takes the form of Metempsychosis, according to which the souls of humans return to bodies, not as eternally blessed humans but as dogs, mules, or peacocks. This is laughable, and if true, it is appalling. Like the Christians, the pagans do have a heaven and hell, namely Elysium and Hades. In the end the pagan is left with the confusing and unattractive possibility that the soul of the deceased evildoer might spend eternity in Hades as a peacock.

I believe we are now at the end of your chilling account of Christian contempt. If we have this contempt in common with you pagans, now it remains only that we compare the ridiculous aspects of our respective convictions. All of our contempt is well-fortified by our convictions, for we believe in the resurrection of the dead. Our hope of resurrection is in fact our disdain for death. Laugh as much as you wish at our misguided minds that die only that they may live. While you are at it, laugh on without restraint and mock with abandon and then take a sponge or even your tongue to blot out the letters where you assert, somewhat as we do, that souls return to bodies. But how much more attractive is our belief, which affirms that the soul returns to the same body! And how much more empty-headed is your tradition to affirm that the human soul takes up residence in the body of a dog or a mule or a peacock.

In the same vein we declare that after death, a judgment is ordained for each man according to his merits. You assign the same judgment to Minos or Rhadamanthos, while rejecting Aristides, a far more just man. This judgment will condemn the wicked to pass eternity in everlasting fire while the pious and the innocent will proceed to a joyous place. According to you the conditions in Hades and in the Elysium are comparable to hell and to heaven. Not only do myths and poetry give this account; the philosophers also confirm the round-trip journey of the soul and the judgment of reward or punishment.

CHAPTER XX

MAY THE PAGANS RECOGNIZE AND

EMBRACE US

This concluding chapter is a classic peroration in the sense that it touches on the main themes of the work and seeks to draw them together into a unified whole. Christians and pagans should extend to each other the hand of friendship, both because they are deeply and inherently similar and because the pagans will correct their errors once they understand that they are in fact even more guilty of the so-called Christian vices than the Christians themselves. Tertullian concludes on a note of enlightened hope. If the pagans could just recognize the actual distribution of truth and error between pagans and Christians, then they would change their ways and become Christians.

O unjust pagans, how long will you refuse to acknowledge your own merits? In fact how long will you continue to disparage them? There is no real difference between us. We are one and the same. Since you in fact cannot hate what you are, then extend your right hand to us, join kisses with kisses, hold us in your embrace, the bloody with the bloody, the incestuous with the incestuous, the conspirators with the conspirators, the contemptuous and the vacant together with their own kind. We have been partners in insulting the gods; we have been partners in provoking their anger.

You too have in your midst a third gender—not so much a third religious persuasion—but a third sex.[1] They are well suited for both male pleasure and for female pleasure, endowed with male and female aptitudes. Do we offend you with this particular shared affinity? Equality lends force to envy. Thus the potter envies the potter and the craftsman envies the craftsman.

But let us put an end now to this make-believe confession. The power of conscience restores the truth and the fixity of the truth. The fact is that all of these charges are true of you alone and they are refuted by us alone. They are launched against us, but when we present an opposing view, your thinking is enlightened, your deliberations are informed, and your judgment is guided. It is your conviction that we should never judge an issue without hearing both sides—the principle that you overlook in the instance of us Christians.

---

[1]   This refers to eunuchs.

You succumb to a defect in your nature, namely that you condemn in others the very vices that you fail to correct in your selves. You have faults of which you know you are guilty and yet you charge them against others. Your stance in life is chaste on the outside and unchaste on the inside. In public you are outspoken about virtue but in private you succumb to vice.

The outrage is that knowing the truth, we are judged by those who do not know the truth and, free of offense, we are judged by those who are guilty. Remove the beam from your own eye so that you may remove the mote from your neighbor's eye. First correct yourselves so that you may punish the Christians. In fact, if you do correct yourselves, you will cease to punish the Christians. Indeed you will be Christians and if you become Christians, you will have transformed yourselves. Learn what you faulted in us and you will cease to find fault. Discover what it is you fail to fault in yourselves and you will find fault.

With these few observations I have offered as far as I can an analysis of your error and a window on the truth. Reject the truth if you can do so after examining it. And then persist in your errors—even if you think you have understood them. But if your chosen path is to love error and to hate the truth, then why not fully acquaint yourself with what you love and with what you hate?

CONCLUSION

This brief presentation of Tertullian's writing does not lead with natural ease into a closing evaluation of his contribution to early Christianity. Intrinsic to Tertullian's thought is the underdeveloped terrain on which Christianity and paganism were becoming acquainted. Tertullian had a troubled awareness of the experiential divergence between Christianity and paganism; moreover, he had not undergone the life-changing journey through conversion that claimed St. Augustine when he gladly followed the Lord's instructions to "take and read *Confessions* VIII.2.29." This conversion gradually ripened into deliverance from a disquieting vision of reality into a state of joyous acceptance. Inherent in Augustine's experience was the overwhelming and irresistible passage into a state of intimacy with the Lord that could not have been imagined until its actual occurrence.

At the time when Tertullian was writing about the Christian experience, almost 200 years prior to St. Augustine's conversion, this type of transformation was not a readily available opportunity for Latin Christians. Implicit in St. Augustine's struggle was a deep longing for intimacy with God. Such intimacy is nowhere in sight in Tertullian's reflections in *On the Testimony of the Soul* or his grim ruminations about the egregious vices presented in the chapter on Rumor (Chapter 7 of *To the Nations*). Tertullian is writing at a moment when intimacy with the Lord is a not a common theme in Latin patristic Christianity. As a consequence we must look for a more oblique disclosure than lies on the surface of the sarcasm, the irony, and the equivocation that characterize the Second Sophistic. One of the major sources of the intrinsic difficulty in Tertullian's expositions is that he is writing at a time when the Latin language lacked the devotional intensity to describe the Christian experience. At times Tertullian's stylistic personality is still very pagan. When he comments on how similar the pagans are to the Christians, he really can include himself on both sides of the equation.